I was on tour with a professional musical group, having acting classes in every city. I came across Matt Zina and he was the best acting coach. He explained things so simply.

Joanne Clifton—*Strictly Come Dancing* Winner

Matt Zina is a multi-award-winning screen-acting coach of over 20 years. Many students of his classes across the UK have gone on to star in prestigious TV shows and Hollywood movies.

He lives and breathes acting. Hailing from a working-class background in Bradford, West Yorkshire, England, he began at the age of eight, gaining roles in some of Britain's best-loved TV series, before finding his true calling as a coach.

The progressive techniques he's developed over the decades have enabled people with no prior experience to become professional working actors in short periods of time.

Matt prides himself on being a disruptor. He never holds back from telling hard truths about acting and what it takes to succeed. He helps his students master not just the skill of acting, but the 'mind-set' and 'business' side of it too.

For a taste of his no-holds-barred wisdom, head to his YouTube channel, social media and podcast.

You'll find all that and more at *https://linktr.ee/mattzina*

To my wife, my saviour, Clare, and my two beautiful children, Megan and Sebastian.
You will forever be my reason.

To all the wonderful people who have supported me throughout this publishing journey.

A special thank-you to Laura, who helped me edit this book into existence and has always been a true friend.

To every single one of you who has trusted me as your acting coach.
Your trust means the world to me and I do not take it for granted.
I owe you all so much.

I am forever grateful for the opportunity to live this amazing life and to dedicate myself to my life's purpose.

This book is for all of you.
xZx

Matt Zina

THE TRINITY ACTING METHOD

AUSTIN MACAULEY PUBLISHERS
LONDON * CAMBRIDGE * NEW YORK * SHARJAH

Copyright © Matt Zina 2025

The right of Matt Zina to be identified as author of this work has been asserted by the author in accordance with sections 77 and 78 of the Copyright, Designs and Patents Act 1988.

All rights reserved. No part of this publication may be reproduced, stored in a retrieval system, or transmitted in any form or by any means, electronic, mechanical, photocopying, recording, or otherwise, without the prior permission of the publishers.

Any person who commits any unauthorised act in relation to this publication may be liable to criminal prosecution and civil claims for damages.

The story, experiences, and words are the author's alone.

A CIP catalogue record for this title is available from the British Library.

ISBN 9781037114380 (Paperback)
ISBN 9781037114397 (Hardback)
ISBN 9781037114403 (ePub e-book)

www.austinmacauley.com

First Published 2025
Austin Macauley Publishers Ltd®
1 Canada Square
Canary Wharf
London
E14 5AA

Table of Contents

Introduction — 9

How to Use the Trinity Acting Method — 16

Part 1: Preparation — 19

Summary — 21

Chapter 1: Emotional Starting-Point (Preparation) — 22

Chapter 2: Physical Starting-Point (Preparation) — 28

Chapter 3: Behavioural Choices (Preparation) — 31

Chapter 4: Scene Type (Preparation) — 36

Chapter 5: Objectives and Tactics (Preparation) — 39

Chapter 6: Personality Traits (Preparation) — 45

Chapter 7: Archetypes (Preparation) — 49

Chapter 8: Tasks (Preparation) — 55

Chapter 9: Learning Lines (Preparation) — 57

Part 2: Method — 63

Summary — 65

Chapter 10: Mantras (Method) — 66

Chapter 11: Objective Desire (Method)	*69*
Chapter 12: Personality and Archetype Discovery (Method)	*72*
Chapter 13: Physicality (Method)	*74*
Chapter 14: Emotional Space (Method)	*77*
Chapter 15: Connection (Method)	*83*
Chapter 16: Belief (Method)	*86*
Chapter 17: Aesthetics (Method)	*89*
Chapter 18: Behavioural Practice (Method)	*92*
Part 3: Application	**95**
Summary	*97*
Chapter 19: Listening (Application)	*98*
Chapter 20: Seeing (Application)	*101*
Chapter 21: Bravery (Application)	*104*
Chapter 22: Behaviour (Application)	*107*
Chapter 23: Tasks Delivery (Application)	*110*
Chapter 24: Beats and Tactics (Application)	*112*
Epilogue—Your Trinity	*115*
Acting Practitioners	*117*
Glossary	*124*

Introduction

Actors think more with their hearts than with their heads.

William Esper

The Trinity Acting Method is a technique I developed to effectively list the different focuses and techniques I was teaching as an acting coach. It was a way of categorising and turning into a definitive method, all of the separate strands of techniques floating around.
This also helped me discover the relationship between all of them and teach my actors how to use these techniques effectively and select them intelligently.

You will find that I have split up this book into three main parts, with the chapters being a sub-category of these parts. The three parts make up the Trinity Acting Method. The Trinity, in its very essence, is quite a simple concept.

It is the three main aspects of an actor's work:

Part 1: Preparation

Everything an actor must delve into the script to discover before the acting process begins as based on the writer's intention. Evidence gathering from the script.

Part 2: Method

Everything an actor must do with all of the information in hand from the preparation stage to the point of beginning the scene. Effectively getting into the correct emotional and physical state, based upon the writer's intention.

Part 3: Application

Everything an actor must be focused on during the scene to give the best version of the scene; again, all based on the writer's intention.

I'm sure you've already noticed the recurring theme throughout this method: The writer's intention. Whilst we can never truly know the full extent of what the writer intended, I'll be teaching you how to find the trace evidence within the text.

This evidence will help you bring more truth to your performance, ensuring that you're supporting the writer in telling their story in the most authentic and powerful way possible.

But first, we need to explore what the role of an actor actually is.

The role of an actor, as a whole, has been on quite a journey over the years. For example, in ancient Greece, an actor would mainly use masks and a strong physical and behavioural presence to present the story of the writer.

From Shakespearian times, whereby the writer himself took absolute centre stage, as to the genius of theatrical works, right through to Victorian theatre, where even then, it was impossible to think of a household name associated with the actor being more prevalent than the writer.

It was around the time of the 'Movie Studios' whereby actors seemed to become a bit too big for their boots. Actors became household names, and writers seemed to shrink into the background. The worst thing that ever happened to this industry, in my opinion, was when the actor took centre stage.

Strange thing to say, but true. Actors have been all too powerful for a long time. Re-writing scripts, creating backstory, even with a fully living, breathing writer in the room! This has made us forget the main purpose of an actor. Worst of all, most actors have seemingly forgotten the purpose of an actor.

An actor is there to purvey the writer's intention as truthfully as the actor is able to. Nothing more, nothing less. That's it!

The problem is, many actors want to feel that they are much more important and therefore, unless they are sat at the end of a production, with a scarf around their neck in the style of Laurence Olivier, spouting about their character's backstory that 'they' created, based on no evidence whatsoever, in a way that sounds impressive to anybody who will listen.

They don't feel they are really an actor. However, I hope this book will show just how much skill it actually takes for an actor to work within this very specific boundary of ensuring that they are purveying the writer's intention with the utmost truth at all times.

As I mentioned before, the idea of the Trinity Acting Method is incredibly simple; however, I am going to show you that each part can contain various different techniques. Some that I would expect an actor to use EVERY time and some that I would expect an actor to select after diligently discovering the purpose of a scene.

After all, the main writer's intention is to tell a story to an audience in a way that the actor needs to pick up on and understand in order to ensure the story gets across to the audience in the best possible way.

From being in this industry for over 25 years as an actor then coach, I have seen a very transient nature to the style of acting, and it appears to formulate a different guise year after year.

This is to do with the writers of TV, film and theatre writing in different styles and the actors having to adapt, as well as with a lot of acting coaches teaching progressive acting methods, which appear to be infiltrating the TV scene particularly.

Another change which seems to be affecting the styles of acting is the more common appearance of the writer and director being the same person. This has led to an absolute need for actors to get on board fully with the writer's intention as it's becoming more common that the writer will be directing them.

It appears, in a way, that over the last five years, acting is returning, kicking and screaming, to a place where it was always supposed to be and I personally feel that this is an incredibly good thing.

A strange thing happened in the UK a little while back. We had a recession and the money went out of the television industry. Suddenly, the types of TV shows being commissioned changed, and a lot of 'cheap-to-make' gritty, northern dramas were being commissioned.

The acting suddenly became incredibly truthful and improvisational and used many of these new writers/directors, including Sally Wainwright and Kaye Mellor. We saw a love of truthful, writer-led acting, which seemed to be mirrored slightly in the US, with many British actors making waves over there with their ability to be both truthful, gritty and, most importantly, believable.

My coaching and the techniques I have developed over a 20+ year career in teaching actors take out a lot of the frustration of the acting coaching I have received in the industry and try to ensure that an actor has both the skill, knowledge, but most of all, the confidence to do all of the things required of an actor. The last of those is the most important.

I specifically remember being in an acting class in Manchester, whereby it was a two-hour class, and the acting coaching was very minimal; however, the modus operandi appeared to be to get the actors into pairs, learn a script for an hour, then for the second hour, have a whole class of actors perform a pair at a time whilst three acting coaches 'rip into them' week after week in front of the class of other individuals.

There wasn't much coaching going on, just lots of 'feedback'. This appears to be a common MO adopted by a lot of acting coaches, and it just has never sat right with me. For instance, a teacher in a normal classroom does NOT teach a mathematical technique by expecting them to know it and apply it.

They spend time teaching the technique, then give the student the confidence to apply the technique effectively, rather than stripping them of confidence in front of their classmates. I genuinely think this is not helpful to an actor, as an actor needs to be incredibly brave and encouraged to take risks.

The skill of an acting coach is to allow an actor to feel safe around giving-in to their instinct whilst at the same time, presenting positive encouragement and technique, coaching them towards progressing as an actor.

A big failure of a lot of acting coaches is the feeling that they can comment subjectively on people's performances in these feedback-type acting coaching classes. They personally might not like it, but Steven Spielberg might.

An acting coach should only ever be commenting on the objective mechanics of the performance. Not what they like or dislike.

With the grounding of ensuring that from day one, the student knows that the actor is but a mere servant of the writer, it ensures that my students are down-to-earth from the very beginning.

This, I feel, has always proved the best way for an actor to progress, and I hope you will get a feel for my acting coaching method whilst reading the various aspects of the Trinity Acting Method in this book.

I know no other way of presenting the information. Just remember, whilst reading all of this information, I am not at any point saying anything that you have been taught is wrong. Acting is a very strange psychological process that humans have adopted to be able to tell stories.

If an actor has certain methods and they genuinely work, then fine. However, from my years of teaching actors, I can genuinely say that I have sifted through many techniques in order to bring you what I believe is the most effective way, in the modern age, to act the writer's intention with as much truth as possible.

There's that phrase again!

How to Use the Trinity Acting Method

When people used to ask what I did, I'd say, 'Oh, I do acting.' Then that shifted to me saying, 'I'm an actor.' It's such a tiny little change in language, but it really feels different.

Bella Ramsey

Now that you know the three parts of the **Trinity Acting Method,** how do you actually use it in practice? Here's a step-by-step breakdown of how to apply the method to improve your acting:

Step 1: Review the Script

Start by diving deep into the script using the **preparation techniques** outlined in chapter 4. Look for clues about the scene type, the writer's intentions and the overall context of the story.

Think about the **director, writer,** and **production house** style. Ask yourself: *What will this scene look like? What's its focus? How does it contribute to the overall story?* This step is about understanding the **output** that's needed from the scene.

Step 2: Select Your Techniques

Once you've understood the scene, assess which **preparation, method** and **application** techniques will help you achieve the desired result. Not every technique is relevant for every scene, so focus on the ones that will bring out the best version of the story.

Step 3: Commit Fully

After selecting your version of the **Trinity,** commit fully to the process. Use the techniques you've chosen to serve the **writer's intention** and execute the scene with absolute truth. Trust your **preparation** and **method** work, and bring it all to life in the **application** phase.

Why the Trinity Acting Method Matters

The Trinity Acting Method isn't about stifling your creativity—it's about channelling it into the right framework. The actor's job is to tell the story in the most authentic way possible, staying true to the writer's intention.

Whether you're working in theatre or screen acting, this method ensures your performance always aligns with the story being told.

Throughout this book, you'll see the Trinity Method broken down further into its individual techniques. As you learn these, remember that acting is a deeply personal process.

You'll adapt and find what works best for you, but always come back to the heart of the method: Serving the writer's story with truth.

Acting is an art, but it also requires discipline and focus. The Trinity Acting Method gives you the tools you need to approach any role confidently and bring it to life, whether on screen or stage.

I encourage you to use this book as a manual. Dip in and out whenever you need it. Come back to it constantly. If your audition isn't going well, whip out this book and apply the Trinity Acting Method.

I want this book to be your lifelong friend, guiding you through an industry that's fun, exciting and challenging. Keep it close—it'll help you navigate every challenge that comes your way!

Part 1
Preparation

Summary

Taking the evidence from the script and making as many notes as possible based on the writer's intention.

Laying the foundation with evidence from the script.

The **preparation** stage is the essential first step in the **Trinity Acting Method.** This phase is all about diving deep into the script to uncover as much detail and insight as possible before you ever step in front of the camera or onto the stage. It's not just about reading the lines—it's about extracting every piece of information the writer has embedded into the text.

In this stage, the actor becomes a detective, analysing the script for clues and evidence that point towards the **writer's intention.** Your job is to gather these insights and use them to build a solid foundation for your performance.

Chapter 1
Emotional Starting-Point (Preparation)

Don't be an actor. Be a human being who works off what exists under imaginary circumstances.

Sandford Meisner

The emotional starting-point is the absolute best place for an actor to prepare a scene and discover information from the text that will be incredibly beneficial for them going forward into the other two parts of the Trinity.

When we are looking at the scene, it is incredibly easy to start looking at the different moments throughout the scene we are preparing, in an attempt to start guessing what we feel we 'should' feel like in each and every moment. However, that is impossible and I will tell you why.

Sanford Meisner had a beautiful quote on acting. He said that an actor should 'be a human being who works off what exists under imaginary circumstances'. However, as an actor, we always feel the need to 'choreograph' our scenes. Planning every moment of it.

I understand this fully. Actors have an awful lot on the line a lot of the time, whether it's an audition, a big scene or a performance. We want to get everything absolutely correct, and being able to choreograph every moment of a scene, helps an actor feel secure.

However, this is not going to help a performance feel truthful. This will not effectively have you, as Sandy put it, 'existing' in imaginary circumstances.

The only thing you can ever really plan for is the emotional starting-point, the emotional space our character finds themselves in at the beginning of the scene before any of the action even takes place.

We find this in the evidence of the scene. We take this instruction from the writer. It comes from a few different sources:

1) The situation and our own understanding of the situation.

If we look at the scene, we can always describe in a nutshell what the circumstances are. A short sentence describing the situation the characters find themselves in. Now remember, we aren't looking for how the character feels mid-scene.

We're identifying how the character feels before the scene. So, if for instance, the circumstance of the scene is that your character is having a confrontation over an unpaid debt, then based on your experience, we can assume that the majority of us and therefore, your character would be nervous leading up to this event.

When you bring your experience of these events to the scene, you also bring an element of you. Which, in terms of acting truthfully, is gold dust. We will come onto this later on, but let me quickly put it like this.

If you are a person who loves confrontation, your experience of this may get you to say that your character is excited. Your experience and your own understanding of a situation will have you choose the emotional starting-point of your character.

2) The description of the character's behaviour in the script.

Behaviour is an aspect of acting I feel is under-represented in many progressive acting methods, but I will champion it throughout this book. Within the script, and attempting to identify how our character feels before the scene, we can look at our character's behaviour that is described at the start of the scene.

If our character, for instance, is described as 'crying and sobbing', we can deduce from that that the character's emotional starting-point is one of grief or upset. Obviously, people cry for all sorts of reasons, but this is why you can use all three of these elements together to ensure that you make the absolute right decision from the evidence.

3) The choice of the language selected by the writer for the character.

Language is a very interesting subject in acting. Every word has a resonance and we emotionally interact with language, whether we are saying it or listening to it. Many actors are incredibly tuned into this and can create spellbinding performances by allowing the words' resonance to affect them in all moments.

What you have to remember is that we select certain words based on how we are feeling. You don't tell someone you love them unless you feel a certain way. You don't scream 'I hate you' unless you are feeling a certain way. You have to use the writer's choice of language to deduce what your character is feeling because of their motivation to use that language.

However, I have to stress that even though we are looking at the language throughout the scene, you are still only using it to see if there is any evidence of how your character feels before the scene begins.

A *study by Alan S Cowen and Dacher Keltner from the University of California recently showed that there are 27 emotions. These are contained within the glossary at the back of this book for your reference.*

Once we have decided exactly how our character is feeling from a combination of the evidential factors above, we note this on our script. Another thing that you should think about is the strength of that emotion.

Say you have decided your character is joyful. You can probably imagine that there is a slight difference between being joyful because someone has made you a cup of tea and joyful because you have just won the lottery. So, you need a system of scale.

I used to use Jacques Lecoq's principle of the seven levels of tension, which is a very interesting principle and one that I fully agree with in terms of his concept. However, for the sake of an actor and a preparation technique, I think the best thing for an actor to do is to rank the level of that emotion between 1 and 10.

You have to be incredibly truthful with this and base it on the full range of human emotion. Grief, for instance, is a tough one. I feel most of us in a civilised country only live between 1 and 8 on the full scale of potential human emotion, not to say there aren't exceptions.

However, we still may be asked to perform a 9 or 10. This scale is quite important because when we are trying to deliver the most truthful performance, we can. Performing a level 9 of excitement whilst going for a meal may not bring about the most believable performance.

Always remember though, this is a personal thing, and whilst you are always working to decide the writer's intention, the writer, in turn, wants you to bring an element of yourself to the role, as this will always go towards creating the most truthful version of the scene.

So, if you personally find going out for a meal in London's West End uber-exciting, then allow your scale to reflect that. So, at this point, you should have marked on your script an emotional starting-point that you have derived from the evidence contained in the script.

Next to it, you should have a number between 1 and 10, based upon your experience of those circumstances that represents the level of that emotion in this context.

As with all of these parts of the preparation section of the Trinity, this information is being gathered to be used during the method and application elements to ensure we are able to give the absolute best and most truthful performance of the script, all using the writer's intention.

The notes you made regarding your character's emotional starting-point will be particularly important in chapter 15.

Chapter 2
Physical Starting-Point
(Preparation)

The gratification comes in the doing, not in the results.

James Dean

The physical starting-point is the physical state the character is in, once again, before the action takes place.

What is someone's physical starting-point?

For instance, if from the scene's evidence, you discover that the character is particularly downhearted and has hit the sofa in a state of depression, it is safe to say that we can understand somebody to be in a particularly lethargic physical state.

However, if we identify someone as stomping up towards someone for a confrontation, one would assume that someone's blood would be pumping.

This is because we are attempting to give the truest portrayal of the writer's intention possible. A big mistake in early actors is to pretend to be out of breath, having been running during a scene.

Well, an actor shouldn't ever be prepared to pretend. An actor wants to exist. So, in the method element of the Trinity, guess what we are going to do? We will, in this instance, make ourselves genuinely out of breath.

In terms of script preparation, I would want an actor to write on their script a brief description of the character's physical starting-point based upon the evidence in the script.

Remember, the reason why we are only talking about the physical starting-point is, as an actor, you are going to go on an 'unplanned journey' through this scene. Therefore anything is possible, both physically and mentally.

So, it could change at any point. For all you know, the other actor could slap you, and you would definitely be in a different physical state then!

Where do we get evidence of the character's physical start-point?

1) The circumstance.

The circumstance and our understanding of the circumstance our character finds themselves in. We look at the circumstance to determine our character's physical state before the scene begins.

Imagine the writer is trying to show a scene where a character is about to be told to 'man up' by his long-term partner. We read the scene, and we see from the evidence; the circumstances are that he is feeling sorry for himself and on the sofa, etc.

We can deduce that his physical state will be one of lethargy. Always describe the circumstances to yourself, as this will always be a good point of reference, particularly for the physical start-point, as there is a very strong, interesting connection between circumstance and our physical reaction to circumstance.

2) The writer's description in the script.

We can be quite lucky at the beginning of the script that a writer will give us a description of our character's physical state. This feels like you have won the jackpot. Nothing else left to do!

3) The narrative

Every now and again, one of the lines may refer to the physical state of the character's physical starting-point. Maybe something along the lines of: 'You've been lying around in bed all day. Isn't it about time you got up? You look lazy; you are lazy'. Again, jackpot!

It doesn't matter how you discover this. Make sure it is based on the evidence that you find somewhere in the script, and write a brief but detailed description of your character's physical state before the scene begins.

Chapter 3
Behavioural Choices
(Preparation)

For me, our job as artists is to serve the story, serve the director and serve the fellow actors. And if you do that, by osmosis, you're serving yourself because you'll get the best out of yourself.

David Oyelowo

Let me break acting down like this; an actor is a vessel to tell a story. The story, in most instances, that a writer is attempting to tell through the actor. The actor tells this story in two main ways. Firstly, the things they say and the lines written by the writer for an actor to say. This is the narrative.

Secondly, an actor tells the story with their behaviour. This isn't particularly given to a great extent by a writer; however, it is the most important factor. The reason the actor's behaviour is more important is an interesting one.

Behaviour is an outward view of how a person is feeling. So, if you have decided how your character is feeling, based upon the writer's evidence, this will start to manifest itself in the scene in terms of the character's behaviour.

Now, here's the interesting bit. What you will find is the reason why behaviour is the most important is that, if you watch very carefully, the way you end up saying your lines is as a by-product of your behaviour.

A good example of this is if I asked an actor to sprint up and down the room 10 times as fast as they can, then ask them to deliver the scene. They will be panting, and the lines will be spaced in a certain way around the breathing patterns; the actor will be in a certain physical state that will make the lines come out a certain way.

Alternatively, if I asked two actors to wrestle over an object and make that the focus of the scene, the lines would be shrieked at certain points, and there would be an element of excitement and fatigue in certain parts.

Effectively, the behaviour will have affected how the lines are said. This is a very much misunderstood concept in our industry. Actors are obsessed with lines.

If an actor goes for an audition, their whole focus tends to be on the lines. If they forget a line, the audition fails in their eyes. Actors fall apart if they get the lines wrong. I have done it myself; I have been in front of a mirror, practising how I think a line should sound.

In many acting classes, it appears that there are script weeks and improvisation weeks. Again, we need to rethink acting.

Every performance is an improvised performance. Why? Because a writer gives us the lines; however, we, as an actor, should always be improvising our behaviour, which, as a by-product, makes the lines be delivered in a very improvisational and therefore, truthful way because how we say our lines should always be a by-product of our behaviour.

So, as part of the Trinity Acting Method, I have stuck to this concept of behavioural choices in the preparation section. So, how do we prepare to improvise behaviour?

Behaviour comes from a few different sources:

1) Our reactions to the others in the scene.
2) Our reactions to the circumstances.
3) Our behavioural manifestation of how we feel.
4) Behavioural choices are given to us by the writer.

Just like in an improvised scene, we can pre-determine some of the behavioural choices we would expect to see from ourselves in the same circumstances our characters find themselves in. As with anything in this preparation section, we are not looking for an actor to choreograph the behavioural reactions and pinpoint when and where they issue them.

But what an actor can do is write a list of behavioural choices they would expect to occur in the scene. So, I would expect from an actor a list of words that describe the behavioural choices they would expect to see from a person, specifically based on their own interpretation of the scene, and on the four behaviour sources listed above.

The more, the better.

Another technique for gathering behavioural choices which I developed in 2021 is the SHOULDA, WOULDA, COULDA technique. This is where we get ideas from different avenues of some behaviours we expect to see.

I get my actors to get a blank sheet of paper and create three columns. The heading of the three columns from left to right would be SHOULD, WOULD and COULD.

SHOULDA—Behaviours and actions we SHOULD see performed. These come from the evidence in the script. If the writer has described it in the script, then you absolutely do it. Make sure you write in this column of your blank piece of paper as many evidenced behaviours and actions as possible that the writer has included in the script.

WOULDA—Behaviours and actions that are based on your own personal life experience or understanding of the circumstances of the scene. What WOULD you do? Write a list of as many behaviours and actions that come to mind in the second column.

COULDA—Behaviours and actions that, if you use your imagination and as long as nobody can turn around and say, "That would never happen," fit the circumstances and really push the boundaries of the scene in a very brave way.

Proficient actors tend to stick to the things that an actor SHOULD do.

Good actors also add on top the things that an actor WOULD do.

Exceptional actors at the top of their game tend to add, on top of all of this, the things that they COULD do.

Obviously, in terms of working practice, we always discuss ideas with a director, but a director tends to want to work with actors that really bring ideas and make things happen on screen. What's the worst that can happen? They shout 'Cut'?

Let me bring up a major point on how all of these particular notes we make actually work in the scene going forward.

The human brain is made of the conscious brain and the subconscious brain. The actor's enemy is the conscious brain.

It's the part that makes an actor feel self-conscious. It's part of the brain that makes them feel nervous.

A performance delivered from this part of the brain usually feels contrived and untruthful. This is part of the brain that may want you to choreograph behavioural choices at certain points across the scene.

The subconscious brain is the actor's best friend. This is part of the brain that just exists truthfully with the circumstances in the scene. It's part of the brain which is 'present' and initiates truthful responses at moments throughout the scene.

A subconscious reaction is a very last-minute decision and we have to play to this. If we make plenty of notes and prep, our subconscious brain will select from these and use one of these behaviours within the scene when an instinct takes us; this is why we still prep the subconscious.

I say it's like computer programming. We are putting all the data in the system, so it is there as a programmed instant response once needed.

Another aspect of behaviour is bravery. It takes much bravery to follow our instinctive behavioural choices.

Chapter 4
Scene Type (Preparation)

Remember: There are no small parts, only small actors.

Constantin Stanislavski

Primarily, an actor's job is to be able to study a scene and break down the writer's will. When working with a director, it is incredibly important and favourable to study the scene to the same extent as them.

The director will have an incredibly good idea of what the writer is trying to convey in the particular scene and, even more importantly, what the writer is trying to demonstrate.

We work on the principle that there are only three types of scenes that fall into the following categories:

1) A scene to show the relationship between characters.

Relationships in acting are incredibly important. It's a big part of storylines. Many scenes are entirely about showing the audience what the relationship between characters is like. This is usually important to the storyline going forward.

So, it is important not to just identify that it is showing the relationship. You should also try to identify what the writer demonstrates about their relationship. Imagine a storyline whereby two siblings' last remaining parent dies, and they are meeting the solicitor to find out what the will may entail for them.

This particular scene wouldn't be half as exciting if there wasn't a scene previously demonstrating that the two siblings struggle to be in the same room together and appear to hate each other. It may be that there is a love triangle, and the writer decides to demonstrate the attraction between two characters.

This will set a story up for all sorts of twists and turns. This is an incredibly common type of scene. Therefore, the relationship between characters is the key part of this scene, and the actors and director should work together to ensure this is the case.

2) A scene to demonstrate something to an audience.

This seems a bit vague, but it is still vital to recognise first that the writer is demonstrating something and then second what that something is. An example of this may be that a pivotal part of a storyline is a character's alcohol addiction.

At some point, this will need to be demonstrated to the audience. The scene may be a wife and husband arguing over her finding his empty bottles hidden around the house. This would effectively demonstrate the issue and give the audience all the information it needs going forward as the story unfolds.

Whatever it is that the writer is demonstrating is the key part of the scene, and again, the actors and director need to work together to ensure this is a key part of the performance of this scene.

3) A scene that moves the story on.

This type of scene is like a full stop or comma. If the writer is building towards a wedding, the wedding must occur. These events must occur if the writer discusses things like a job interview or a romantic date. It is effectively a scene that we expect to happen that moves the story from one place to the next.

So, there we have it. Three categories that every one of our scenes should fit into. I would expect an actor to make a note on their script as to which type of scene it is and, in case of the first two categories, what it is specifically that they are demonstrating.

This will come in particularly useful when identifying the most relevant parts of the Trinity Acting Method to use in order to get the best out of the scene for the audience.

Chapter 5
Objectives and Tactics
(Preparation)

Acting is standing up naked and turning around very slowly.

Rosalind Russell

This is an incredibly big subject and will require a lot of explaining. Stanislavski pointed out that every human being would walk around mute unless they needed to achieve something.

The very act of needing to achieve something gives us the need to speak, behave in a certain manner or make behavioural choices. Standing before a class, I ask, "What am I trying to achieve now in talking to you all?"

They say I am trying to get them to learn. But when you break it down, they could guess that because of my demeanour shown with my voice and behaviour. I am raising my voice to be heard by all and deliver what I am saying with authority.

I am making gestures and meeting the eyes of all the students in the room. I ensure the information gets across with every ounce of my human ability. Why? Because as a human, once I know what I want to achieve, I instinctively use every ounce of my expressive self to achieve it. I have an inner need and I call this an objective. Your objective instructs you how to act!

In order to appear both truthful and real, we should really be acting with an objective within a scene.

I would suggest that to get to an objective in a scene, we should first understand what our character is doing in the scene. Now, this is important because we are never actually working out what our character's objective is.

The objective is a personal thing. Every one of us operates different objectives in our own lives. We operate on certain objectives more than others.

So really, we identify from the writer's intention, what exactly our character is doing in the scene and then work out our objective based on what we find. This is, therefore, the best way to bring a huge element of ourselves to the character.

To break it down further, let's look at a scene between two characters. We find that two neighbours appear to disagree with the placement of a fence.

You would then work out very simply what your character is doing. You will find this from the writer's chosen language for the character. Usually best identified when you just read your character's lines only.

In this instance, you may find that your character is 'venting' his frustration on the other person. Notice that this will always be a verb. A doing word ending in 'ing'.

You then ask yourself, why is my character venting? What would I be trying to achieve if I were venting at someone? However, you are no longer thinking about the scene; you are thinking about your own life.

Go back to the last time you did what your character was doing, then ask yourself, what was I trying to get the other person to do? For example, the last time that I 'vented' on someone, I was attempting to get them to 'snap'. This then becomes my objective.

Here are some common objectives that I use with my students.

To Help Me
To Save Me
To Go Away
To Understand
To Play
To Bite
To Get on Side
To Get on Board
To Crack
To Break
To Crumble
To Surrender
To Laugh
To Smile
To Battle
To Be Reassured
To Snap
To Be Wound up
To Man Up
To Submit
To Melt
To Back Down
To Squirm

To Blush
To Get a Grip
To Like Me
To Love Me

Notice that these common objectives are short, sharp emotive phrases. This is really useful in the next stage of using an objective within a scene. Many actors tend to want to give big explanations of their character's objective.

However, it is much simpler and more effective to get an objective which is personal to you and that you would absolutely be attempting to achieve if you were doing what your character is doing.

Returning to my example of getting someone to snap if I was venting. This is what I would genuinely be trying to get another person to do in this situation. If this was at the heart of my performance, and I had in mind that I needed to achieve this with every ounce of my soul, then it would affect how I said the lines.

It would affect my behavioural choices. It would affect my whole demeanour in the scene. That is why objectives in scenes work so well and create an element of personal truth in a scene.

I would expect two things to be written at the top of an actor's script. What the character is doing and therefore, what our objective is.

There is another element to this that we can prepare for; however, the main part of this will be looked at in the application section of the Trinity Acting Method. Good old tactics!

What do I mean by tactics?

It's quite a simple concept really, and children are amazing at this. When they want something, they tend to try every tactic in the book. Imagine when you were a teenager, and you wanted some money from your mother to go to the cinema.

Your objective is to get your mother to crack or give in. She says no. So, your first tactic is to get angry and storm out. That has no effect. You come back a while later and tell your mum she looks nice.

She says, "I know what you're doing; the answer is still no." You then start to cry. She relents and gives you some money! A common occurrence in many households around the world.

However, you will notice from this example that even though there was one overall objective, the child used different tactics to attempt to achieve that objective; flattering, shouting, crying and manipulating.

Notice they are all verbs.

This is exactly the same for you within a scene. Once you have your objective, work out the ways in which you would attempt to achieve that objective by writing down as many verbs (doing words that end in 'ing') as you can.

Earlier, I offered an example of an argument over a fence. My objective was to get the other person to snap. If I asked myself to identify the different tactics I would employ to get someone to snap, I would say that my tactics would be 'afflicting', 'belittling', coaxing' and 'disheartening'. Again, notice how all of these words are verbs. I call them acting verbs or tactical verbs.

Note that I am not going to choreograph these tactics into my script and decide at which moments I am going to take on these various tactics. Once noted on your script, this is now for the application section and will eventually be an instinctive decision during the scene.

So, once again, I would expect you to have some notes on your script of some tactics that you would employ to attempt to achieve the overall objective.

Chapter 6
Personality Traits
(Preparation)

The more personal, the more universal.

Gary Ballinger

When we are watching acting, I sometimes think that the main factor that we are entertained by is the interest we find from seeing different personalities find themselves in different circumstances.

We marvel at how they cope, respond and behave. Personality is important and the main focus of the casting process, the director's brief and the writer's vision.

A big mistake made by many actors at castings is the inability to take the circumstances that are written and just freely allow their own personality to play outside the scene and therefore, allow us to see how they would cope, respond and behave within the circumstances presented by the writer. Because, as I said previously, that's the entertaining and interesting part of all of this.

I often have actors, sometimes even in their first class, telling me that they don't want to be type-cast and always want to play different characters. This is a very classic old-fashioned notion.

We don't just play out one aspect of our personality constantly. We are incredibly complex beings. We have many associated personalities and we play them out across all sorts of different circumstances throughout our lives.

We may act polite and charming in front of our 'in-laws', but then raucous and outlandish with our close circle of friends. This is something we need to recognise and in some ways, I encourage actors to watch themselves and, in some cases, laugh at themselves, but mostly identify the different personality traits that we possess.

Because in the end, when we understand the truth of ourselves, we can bring this understanding of the truth of ourselves in different circumstances and be aware that we are bringing the utmost truth to a role.

So, what is a personality trait?

Also known as a characteristic; however, a characteristic is more associated with a quality that may have been built or absorbed by a person, whereas a trait is something you are deemed to just possess organically, even hereditary.

You can see I also used the word 'quality', which is also freely used to describe the same thing. For the simplicity of your understanding, I will just use the word characteristic going forward. As they're both similar enough to be used interchangeably for our purposes.

An actor's major task is attempting to identify which characteristic will work best within a scene at any particular time. We are effectively identifying which aspect of our personality should be in play in the circumstances of that particular scene. Notice I said our personality, not the characters.

With this, I like to employ a modern theory that I have observed and developed; the Theory of Reflection.

In essence, this is a very simple theory which is inherent in our everyday life. When we look at others, we identify their characteristics, sometimes without even speaking to them. When we do this, we are transposing ourselves onto them and then picking out what we see.

We mainly see characteristics in others that we ourselves have. For example, if we haven't trained as ballet dancers, we wouldn't be able to recognise a plie or a pirouette; however, when you are familiar with something, we instantly do.

In the same way, if we are familiar with certain characteristics, we will see them played out in another person, it's also a fantastic way of identifying characteristics we all share.

However, we need to take a script and apply this theory to identify our own characteristics and apply it to the scene. Very simply, read the scene, the circumstances, the lines, and from what you have read, note down as many characteristics you feel you have seen displayed in your character.

It may look like this:

Forthright
Bullish
Charming
Self-Assured

If you do this instinctively, what you will find is that the list you have developed will be terrifying! Because inadvertently, you have described aspects of your personality. I certainly have, reading back the list above.

This is a beautiful little technique, very simple but very effective.

Now that you will have a few characteristics noted down, I will document, in the 'method' part of the Trinity Acting Method, how to use and select these characteristics in order to create the most truthful performance, showing your personalities response to the circumstances of the scene.

Chapter 7
Archetypes (Preparation)

If you really do want to be an actor who can satisfy himself and his audience, you need to be vulnerable.

Jack Lemmon

So, we have looked at personality traits/characteristics and discovered that we have many, many different characteristics that make up who we are and we can pick and choose these and bring them to our truthful existence within a scene.

This is still important because the next subject is very similar and interlinked.

We next turn our attention to an incredibly interesting subject that helps us understand ourselves in even more detail and takes a lot of work and research over a certain period to get right.

When it comes to casting, you are to be cast in a literary role. There is no getting away from it; you are literally being cast as an archetypal literary role that we can imagine has been written down time and time again. This is known as an archetypal character.

If you think of it as every type of character, you might find in a written piece of work. A script, novel, poem, anything really. So from the list, you would see classic literary characters like 'hero' and 'matriarch' right through to modern day archetypal characters like 'chav' or 'hipster' that we see in so many current dramas.

This is, of course, an evolving document as, year after year, more and more and more archetypal characters are written.

How does this relate to an actor?

Well, with these archetypal characters, although they are written in literature, they are also taken from everyday life and therefore are a representative parallel of archetypal humans out there also.

We will find that we are one of these archetypal characters in real life, and if we discover who we are, we can turbo-boost our casting opportunities and our understanding and application of ourselves to the roles we are going for and playing.

So, how do we discover which archetype we are?

Well, for a start, I've lied to you. We are not discovering just one archetype; the average human has various archetypes. I like to work on four distinct archetypes that develop from four distinct places in our personal evolution.

From years of looking at this particular subject, I have identified four ways to identify where our archetypes come from. When you look at these, I would like you to compare them with the archetypes list from the glossary and add one of the words that best describe each of these.

1) An archetype that you genuinely have that you are most ashamed of.

This is particularly difficult and takes a lot of honesty. However, this is your strongest archetype and it will create a performance which will be full of 'vulnerability', as it has you laying out a part of yourself that you usually are not comfortable with.

That discomfort comes across as vulnerability on screen. It may be that you work out that in a lot of situations, you are a 'coward', and you hate that about yourself. It may be that you realise that you always seem to set yourself up as the victim and outwardly transmit that, and you wish you didn't. Honesty here will go an awful long way.

2) An archetype that comes from your profession or daily activity.

This is something you do on a daily basis, so it is a big part of who you are. It may be that you are in the care profession, so you have developed into a 'caregiver' or you are a teacher, so naturally, this becomes a big part of you.

A 'teacher' is therefore your very archetype. You may be a full-time mother, so therefore, have become a 'matriarch' within your family.

3) An archetype that comes from a relatively recent change in your life.

This is an interesting one, but you will find that if you have suddenly decided to take on your wish of becoming an actor, you may be a 'dreamer'. Maybe you are on a get-fit drive and feel you have become an 'Olympian'.

Find an interesting archetype that best represents this. I always give the fact I laugh at the change in my archetypal character because when I was 18 with a previous 'seeker' archetype, I would look at the opposite sex on evenings out and think: *Wow, how amazing does she look!*

Now that I am a father and a husband and have more of a 'caregiver' archetype, I'm more likely to think: *She must be freezing in that attire!* This is a shining example of how we constantly change and develop as people.

4) An archetype you have always had as long as you can remember that you have never been able to break from.

This is a difficult one. It may be that, like me, when you were a child, you couldn't just have one chocolate biscuit; you had to have the whole box. You may have drank too much through your twenties and still overdo certain behaviours now. That would make you an 'addict'.

You may have never liked to take the limelight and have always been happier playing second-fiddle to someone. That would make you a 'side-kick'. Just remember you have never been able to shift this archetype. It has followed you throughout your life.

Remember, even once you have found these four main archetypes you possess, they are always likely to change as you develop as a human, so make sure you repeat this process and constantly think about these in order to ensure they are up to date.

How do we select which archetype to bring out in the scene?

Well, an archetype can contain many different personality traits/characteristics. So, I would like you to repeat what you did in chapter 6, whereby you discovered as many words that describe your characters' characteristics', using the 'Theory of Reflection'.

You will find that the majority of the characteristics you have written down for the character you are playing will fit mostly into one of the archetypes you have written down.

For example, my four main archetypes are as follows:

1) Bully
2) Prophet
3) Caregiver
4) Addict

The examples I gave for the list of characteristics in the previous chapter were as follows:

1) Forthright
2) Bullish
3) Charming
4) Self-Assured

So, looking at the above characteristics, it turns out that all of those characteristics work incredibly well with my 'prophet' archetype. My job as an acting coach effectively sees me 'prophetise' the research I have done over many years.

You will find that these are the characteristics I seem to employ when I am within that particular archetype. I am forthright and bullish in nature, but with an element of self-assuredness and charm (hopefully!).

So, for this particular character, I would take forward this archetype into the second part of the Trinity Acting Method.

Once you have these archetypes absolutely nailed to the mast, you will find that you look at a script and start to instantly recognise which of your four archetypes will be best to use.

Make a note of which archetype you are going to use on your script.

Chapter 8
Tasks (Preparation)

The first step to a better audition is to give up character and use yourself.

Michael Shurtleff

In acting, it is a constant battle to get actors to keep their minds off the words that they are saying. Remember, how the words end up being presented is a by-product of the actor's behaviour.

One of the oldest and most effective techniques of an acting coach is to give an actor a task to complete and therefore, with the actor effectively concentrating on the task, the only space for the words to appear is from an actor's instinct. This makes the narrative appear more truthful and the words then become a by-product of the task.

A task is very much like behaviour, but I deal with it separately from behaviour as it is important in the preparation section of the Trinity Acting Method to ensure you are discovering and looking at it slightly separately; as for one thing, a task has various behavioural off-shoots that could come from one task.

Imagine the scene: One character is attempting to read the other character's diary; in essence, the two characters end up fighting over possession of the diary at the same time as the lib is taking place.

Now, a lot of the time when I see a scene like this, a common mistake is that the actors will say a line, do a bit of grabbing for the book, pull away, say the line and then have a go at trying to grab the book.

The trick in scenes where there is a definitive task given to you by the writer is to fully commit to the task and allow that to be the basis and aim in a scene for however long you are instructed by the script that it takes place.

As with the above mentioned scene, the actors are fully committed; they get out of breath, the grunts and the ad-libs associated with the task fly out with vigour, as well as that their lines come out in a timely and truthful manner alongside the scene and guess what?

It's all truthful and the actor literally exists within this scene. Sometimes, acting is just knowing where to put your concentration to give the most truthful and realistic effect.

So, as a preparation technique, I would expect my actors to discover, based on the evidence of the script, whether their character in the script is undertaking a task within the scene. I would then ask an actor to make a note of it on their script.

Chapter 9
Learning Lines (Preparation)

The best acting is instinctive. It's not intellectual, it's not mechanical, it's instinctive.

Craig MacDonald

There are so many ways to learn lines and every actor has their own way. The way I want to deal with this is to allow you to understand the psychology of learning lines and how to work out your method around this understanding.

The mind is a strange thing. It is well-documented that, as humans, we appear to use very little of our brains. A strange thing that I have discovered is that just like a muscle, you can train the mind to become better at learning lines with practice. The more you do it, the easier it gets.

I would also like to add, at this stage, that for the purpose of this method of acting, I expect the lines to be so well-learnt that they are 'instinctive' and therefore require very little thought at the performance stage.

As you can see with a lot of the points I have already laid down, the words and the way in which they are said is secondary to behaviour. Therefore, if your mind is constantly on the lines, the scene becomes contrived.

The truth comes when the lines emerge 'instinctively' and follow your human behaviour. Under the great Sanford Meisner's tutorship, when a scene wasn't going so well for actors, he would have them go to a private place and just run the lines as fast as possible, with absolutely no acting until they were instinctive.

Then, they could return and put their thought processes in the correct places. I sometimes watch actors perform, and I see them literally physically look upwards into their own heads to collect their lines, and they are disconnected and out of the scene instantly, ruining all of the hard work they have put into the scene.

From my perspective, the first instruction is never act when learning lines. Flat read. If you do, you start to make decisions around how you want to say these words that will run into the scene when you actually perform, and you want to be free at this stage. Only start acting once you have been through the first two stages of the Trinity Acting Method. Be patient.

The second point I want to raise is a strange one: We read a script once or twice, and our brain knows it off by heart. It's just that quite a lot of things get in the way of you accessing it.

The first thing that gets in the way is the script itself. It becomes a 'comfort blanket' for a lot of actors. Put it down at the earliest opportunity. The neurological pathway that needs to access what, as we have discussed, is already in your head; you will not access it fully until it understands that you don't intend to use the script any more.

Put it down and only pick it up if you can't improvise through it, ad-lib or you go blank. Once you are back on track, put it down again.

In my classes, I am very strict with my actors in this regard and I train them to learn scripts fast. The brain is like a muscle and it can get incredibly quick at learning lines.

The second thing that gets in the way is the way in which we start to learn it. We are trying to get every word absolutely correct. Our brain over-analyses and makes us anxious that we are getting it wrong.

I say, in the first instance, as a tip, to be improvisational with every read. Then, at the end of the read, look at it and see where you can 'tighten up'. To put my actors at ease, I am often heard to mention that 'I never trust an actor that gets a script word-perfect'.

If they are being truthful, then they will always bring an element of ad-lib or change a word to how they would say it. So, be improvisational and then tighten up as you go along.

If you are lucky enough to have someone to learn your lines with, I run with a technique that I have honed over a few years that seems to get the best results.

In a two-hander, for instance, actor 'A' will learn the line from the page and then look up and say it aloud to actor 'B'. Actor 'B' has been watching them all of this time. However tempting it is to look down at the script.

Actor 'B' will now look at the script and learn their next line whilst looking at the page, then look up and say the line to actor 'A', who has been watching them all of that time. The benefits of this are:

1) You learn the lines one by one as you go along.

When you have anything difficult to do, it is always best to break it down into little bits. That's what you are doing here.

2) You are watching and listening to each other, seeing and hearing cues, and getting into the spirit of being reactionary.

It is getting you into the correct mind-set of understanding that your job is to watch the other person, react and not spend all of your time with your head in the script, ignoring the other person.

3) You learn the script faster.

As with point one, you aren't learning it all at once. You are also watching and listening, so you hear the cues and don't miss the important information that will help you access the lines.

The strange thing about the way that scripts are written is that they are usually written as a conversation. The next line is often the only thing possible to say as a reply. So, the answer a lot of the time is to just listen!

When an actor fails to listen to the previous line because they are in their own head, trying to remember the next line, this is when they fail because they don't pick up on the cue for what they should be saying.

If you are on your own, there are many techniques out there. Recording the other part of the conversation is an incredibly popular one, along with some new line learning apps that are popping up on IOS and Android.

If you can get help, which actors always need, I would insist that an actor of mine go with my script technique. As part of my classes, I encourage a community spirit amongst my actors with WhatsApp groups, etc. to ensure that should they need to learn lines or have a self-tape, they are always willing and able to help each other.

Once again, I want to reiterate that it is of prime importance that these lines are learnt to the stage that they are instinctive and require minimal thought. Once you're at this stage, you can move on to the method element of the Trinity.

Part 2
Method

Summary

Everything an actor needs to do to be physically and emotionally ready for when they hear 'action'.

Preparing your body and mind for the scene.

The **method** stage of the **Trinity Acting Method** is where all the preparation work you've done starts to come alive. Now that you've gathered evidence from the script and fully understood the **writer's intention,** it's time to bring that information into your body and emotions, ensuring you're fully prepared for the moment the director calls 'action'. This stage is about connecting the intellectual work of the **preparation** phase to your physical and emotional state, so you can deliver a truthful performance.

In this phase, the actor's focus shifts from analysis to embodiment. It's the process of getting into the right emotional and physical state for the scene, so that when the cameras start rolling, you are completely present in the moment, ready to respond truthfully to the circumstances of the scene.

Chapter 10
Mantras (Method)

Acting is not about being someone different. It's finding the similarity in what is apparently different, then finding myself in there.

Meryl Streep

A mantra is a fantastic tool. Used by actors to create some fantastic effects. Mantras, in fact, go back thousands of years. It is the understanding that you can change your human state of mind by repeating a statement internally in your head.

Buddhist monks do it when meditating; in fact, you will find you do it in your everyday life. When you tell yourself, 'It will be okay' or you get super angry, you decide to 'calm down'. We decide we need to change the state of our mind, so we repeat something in our head until we truly believe it, and it enters our consciousness and becomes behaviour.

As a method, I would like you to take what you have decided is your character's emotional starting-point and this is what we will use to get ourselves a plausible mantra to work with.

So, maybe you decided that your character was joyful to the level of 5/10. I want you to take your script and write a line before your actual first line takes place. The rules of this line that you write are this:

* It has to reflect your character's emotional starting-point.
* It has to reflect the level that your character is feeling the emotion.
* It has to be in your own words. The language that you would use.
* It has to be emotive. Something that will genuinely get you feeling the way your character feels from the evidence contained.
* Be simple/cheesy. Nobody is ever going to hear this line!

For instance, your first line is 'I have something to tell you'.

Then, based upon all of the factors above, the fact that I am joyful to the extent of a 5/10, using my own language. I would write the line:

'I'm absolutely bursting with happiness; I can't wait to tell you.'

As cheesy as this actually is, it absolutely does the job. I cannot say it repeatedly without it making me feel joyful and giving me impetus into the scene.

Remember, not many scenes start from the beginning. We drop in halfway through most of the time. We certainly drop in halfway through the character's experience and therefore, to start neutral and work your way into every scene does not make you appear truthful.

You are already invested in these emotions, and this will cause the impetus for your actual first line to appear truthful.

What do I want you to do with this line?

When you are about to begin your first line, you will repeat the mantra line over and over again in your head, allow it to fill up your whole consciousness and allow it to fill your emotion; when you finally hear 'action' or begin your scene, you will begin by saying the scripted line.

However, this mantra will have had the effect of causing your first line and therefore, the rest of the scene to be incredibly truthful from this point onwards. Allow it to affect the way the mantra fills out into your behavioural choices, the decision you make and the way you engage with your fellow actors.

Make sure you are incredibly driven by this mantra and take it on into the application element of the Trinity.

Chapter 11
Objective Desire (Method)

Good acting—real acting is impossible to spot. Do you ever catch talents like Robert Duvall or Kathy Bates acting? No. I defy you to show me where.

William Esper

We looked at how to take the writer's intention and turn it into tangible objectives that we would want to achieve in that scene. Effectively, we personalised the objectives and made them our own.

It is incredibly important that once we have these objectives in our scene that we emotionally connect with them.

The common objectives that I listed, you may notice, were short, sharp, punchy, yet emotive words. Now, my advice is this. If you don't feel the objective on any emotional level, then change it.

Maybe it doesn't excite you? Scare you? Get you angry? Then it means it hasn't hit you where it needs to, so you have no emotional resonance with it. CHANGE IT!

The main reason you would have an emotional connection with an objective is that you mainly find yourself doing this particular objective a lot. Therefore, it has harboured a lot of emotion for you and you have a lot of emotional connections around it.

You will also find that you will narrow down objectives to a few you regularly use as you start to recognise that these are the ones you do regularly in your own life.

In this method element, how do you warm up your objective?

Well, if you are with a fellow actor and you have the opportunity, I ask my actors to stand opposite their partner and look at each other and say their objective in this way.

Person A: "I am going to get you to (insert objective)."
Person B: "I am going to get you to (insert objective)."

I encourage them to improvise and 'riff' around these lines, I get them to keep repeating over and over, and I ensure that they genuinely get into a competition with their fellow actor to be the one that appears to truly mean it the most.

I get them to use each other names so they ground it within the moment and personalise it. But the most important thing is that I get them to truly emotionally connect with their objective like it's the most important thing in their life.

I then shout 'action', and they always discover that their performance is alive and dynamic, based on the belief they have in their objectives. But we can only do it like this in rehearsal; we can't do this on set or alone.

So, the best way to do it personally is to turn the above exercise into a mantra. Repeat in your head. *I will get you to (insert objective).* I would say always look at someone, or if you are not with a fellow actor, imagine their face or faces.

But again, the single most important thing is to ensure that you are connected to the objective on a deep emotional level.

Make sure that you go after this objective 'fiercely' and ensure that you bring in a range of 'tactics'. Basically, the different ways in which you are to go about achieving this objective.

Another thing to remember in this particular element is that it is a competition; your fellow actor is attempting to beat you and achieve their objective just as you are trying to achieve yours.

What transpires in the middle is what critics, viewers and people in our industry refer to as 'chemistry'. It's basically all of the chemical reactions that 'spark' off as actors compete with each other as they try and achieve their objectives.

Chapter 12
Personality and Archetype Discovery (Method)

Conflict is what creates drama. The more conflict actors find, the more interesting the performance.

Michael Shurtleff

After discovering first whether you are going to use a personality trait in the scene or press forward a complete archetype, it turns out that, luckily, they both have a very similar technique by which you can get physically and psychologically ready.

So, you need to focus on the particular personality trait or archetype you have discovered that you feel serves this scene. Then, close your eyes and retreat into your consciousness. I would like you to view yourself under the guise of the particular personality trait or archetype you have elected to use.

See how you behave, how you interact with other people, how you seem to react to stimuli around you, the choices you make, how you talk, how you walk, really get the detailed picture in your head.

This is a very old-fashioned technique, but one that serves. Once you feel you have seen every detail of that 'version' of yourself, I want you to imagine stepping into your own shoes. Go from viewing that person to becoming that person. In essence, that person is you, so it should feel incredibly natural to become that 'version' of yourself.

Then, stay inside that version of yourself and try and maintain it until you hear 'action'.

Another tip that my actors find incredibly useful is to 'step inside' the particular version of themselves that matches the character and keep within it for the entirety of an audition, including the 'chat' and greeting.

There are a few incredibly important things to focus on with this particular technique. The main aspect of your personality is your behaviour. Ensure that your personality/archetype emerges mainly through your choices/behaviour.

Make sure you are free and brave, open and, in every moment, instinctive with your behavioural choices. This is the most sure-fire way that you will lean on a particular part of yourself whilst acting out the scene.

Let's face it. We watch a dramatised performance, regardless of what format, because we are somewhat perversely interested in how different types of people (personalities/archetypes) engage with different circumstances.

So, it is incredibly important that an aspect of you is front and centre in your performance, and to reiterate, your personality is the choice you make.

Chapter 13
Physicality (Method)

That's what makes acting so attractive.
You get to break all your own rules.

Gerardine Clark

A really crude and simplistic way in which I like to introduce the concept of 'method' is by stating that it is effectively ensuring that you do everything you can to ensure you are physically and mentally prepared for the moment you hear 'action' and the scene begins.

So, to this end, physicality is an incredibly important subject in this particular section of the Trinity.

The way to think about this is very simple. We use the writer's intentions and the evidence to discover our characters' physical state, based upon circumstances and all sorts of factors which we investigate and come to the most truthful conclusion.

We then need to ensure that we aren't going to pretend to be in this physical state. We ensure that we fully commit to genuinely having this physical state to take into our scene.

Jack Nicholson, on the set of *The Shining*, is the most well-known example of this. In his famous scene where he delivers the famous line 'Here's Johnny', Jack understands that his character is pumped up; he understands that to make this look truthful, his body should be giving off the genuine physical outward signs of someone who has been physically running, is 'super-charged' and excitable.

The outward signs of this are physical sweat, a red, flushed face and a body responding very rapidly with the blood pumping. How did he achieve this?

Famously, there are videos out there that show him using a punch bag behind the camera. Screaming and running on the spot. Therefore achieving physical sweat, a red, flushed face and a body that's responding very rapidly with the blood pumping.

We need to plan for the physical state we must achieve from scene to scene. You need to have this conversation with the director to ensure you have any facilities available to ensure you are absolutely bringing about the writer's intentions.

Remember that your body is a tool and is incredibly important. If you get injured, it will hold back production. So, ensure you stretch and warm up; take this incredibly seriously. As this is your livelihood and injuries can be a massive setback.

Remember that physicality is not just high action if a character has just got out of bed. What does that look like? How would you replicate that?

You would expect to see someone with low energy, relatively pale as the blood isn't pumping, slow reactions and movement with tired eyes and features.

Obviously, make-up can replicate a lot of this; however, you would need to try and replicate it physically. This is the time to be still and make yourself tired by closing your eyes for large periods of time. Focus on the feeling of being tired and make yourself yawn.

One of the most wonderful things about the human body is this. Whenever you replicate the physicality of a feeling or an emotion, your brain catches up and genuinely starts to respond.

As an exercise, I want you to yawn, be still and close your eyes. You will instantly see that you start to feel tired regardless of whatever physical state you were in previously. The human body is truly astounding and you have full control over it.

If you want to tell the absolute truth in these scenes, this particular method element is constantly overlooked by actors but genuinely is the icing on the cake. It's the bit that impresses those around you.

It's the technique that shows to the production crew and director that you are working hard towards the good of the production, but most of all, it shows that you know your job. This is a much under-used, under-thought-out, yet important element of the acting method.

Chapter 14
Emotional Space (Method)

The more personal, the more universal.

Gary Ballinger

One of an actor's most fundamental yet basic techniques is to effectively work out from the script how your character feels and then show an audience these emotions during a scene.

There are all sorts of methods for this particular concept. Ranging from Stanislavsky to Lee Strasberg and his 'emotional memory', which was a popular movement in years gone by.

However, I always feel that so many acting coaches or 'practitioners' have always looked to overcomplicate what is, in essence, a very simple idea. I am going to attempt to simplify it for you.

I asked you to identify your character's emotional starting-point. This is how your character feels before they even say a word before the event.

It is now up to us as an actor to understand that to create a performance that translates well to screen, we have to not 'pretend' to have that particular emotion but genuinely have that emotion.

We will effectively use methods to get ourselves into this emotional space so that we can take into our scene at the point of hearing 'action'. As I mentioned previously, this has been a subject that has been overcomplicated over many years. I can simplify it like this:

We get an emotional response from any stimulus we focus our senses on.

So effectively, as long as we know what emotional start-point we need to reach, we need to focus our senses on whatever we know will give us the desired emotional response. Just remember that we also have different levels of emotions.

I asked you to also come up with a number between 1 and 10 that distinguished the emotion level. So effectively, your stimuli also have to give you the strength of emotion required. I like to call it reverse-engineering.

So, for instance, if we have decided from deciphering the script that our character is feeling angry coming into this scene, we need to make ourselves genuinely angry to play out the scene with maximum truth. You have so many options at this point that it is untrue. You have to identify what works best for you.

Firstly, what stimulus are we going to use?

Will you use something auditory, like a song that gets you riled up and angry? Are you going to use something visual, like a colour that angers you? Are you going to use memory from the past? Are you going to use something happening in the present that is making you angry?

Are you going to focus on something in the future that you know you have coming up that is going to give you the emotional response required?

It actually doesn't matter what stimulus you use. But realise and even practice. Everything we focus on in life gives us an emotional response. My mother always says, "Don't paint a room blue; it will make you feel depressed." My God, she's right. As even looking at a colour gives you an emotional response.

But all of the ideas I mentioned above are about you selecting the best stimulus which is going to work best for you to genuinely make you feel how you have deduced your character feels. But it doesn't work unless you fully engage your senses also.

If you choose a song, you have no choice but to engage your hearing. If you look at something in the present, like a person or a colour, you cannot help but engage your vision. However, let us unpack the box, which is using 'recall' or memories or using your mind to think about things in the present or the future.

I have an exercise that I do with my students. It's called the wooden box. I ask my student to neutrally walk around the space, thinking purely about the emotional starting-point they wish to achieve. I then get them to stand still in space and close their eyes. I then go through these steps:

1) Imagine that there is a wooden box, and inside that box is every single one of your past memories, thoughts, events, past, present, future, the good, the bad, the ugly, the forgotten, the pushed-out. I say that

when it comes to acting, everything is on the table to be used.

2) I imagine the key has a lock and they have the key in their back pocket. They then have to take the key, open the box physically, put it back in their pocket and open the lid.

3) They then have to imagine searching around in the box for the memory, which will give them both the emotion that they require and the level they require.

4) Once they have found a memory that will be their stimuli, they will then start to engage vision as their initial sense, as they will start visualising the event.

5) The brain is amazing, so I remind them that they can engage so many more senses with memories/events in their mind (touch, sound, smell and taste). This will really get them to have an emotional response to the mental stimuli they have selected.

6) I ask them that once this stimulus is working for them and they have engaged all of their senses with it, they then open their eyes and allow that emotion to dictate their behavioural responses, their instincts and impulses and get them to move around the room with these things at the forefront of their existence.

7) I then usually shout 'action' at this point and get the actors to find their partners and deliver their scene.

In this exercise, my actors usually find an incredible increase in the truth around their scenes. They usually love how their scene goes, how they feel the genuine emotions and the lines feel like they come out as they were meant to.

But there's one final step. A very important one.

8) At the end of the class or the scene, I get them to close their eyes again and imagine the wooden box. I insist that they imagine the thought/event/memory go back into the box, and they then physically close the lid and lock it back up again, sliding the key into their back pocket.

Why do I do this? Mental health is incredibly important, and I have to ensure the welfare of my students. This simple technique helps them pack off any memory that they use and put it firmly away, away from their present conscious mind.

I could easily write an entire book on the mental health and well-being of actors. But for now, I just want to urge you to **take care of yourself.** Make sure you integrate this particular exercise into your technique and don't overlook it—doing so could have serious consequences for you down the line. Your mental health is just as important as the work you do.

The final thing I wanted to touch upon is when I said previously, "The lines feel like they come out as they were meant to."

What do I mean by this?

Well, the main place we get our evidence from when discerning the emotional starting-point is the language the writer selects. Suppose the writer is, as we have used as the main example in this chapter, wanting to show their character as angry. He will select the language that a person would only use when they are angry.

So, therefore, until we genuinely make ourselves feel the same way as our character, the writer's selected words can never truly feel comfortable coming out of our mouths.

Suddenly, when we work on getting to the correct emotional start-point to the correct level, they do. Usually to great effect also!

Chapter 15
Connection (Method)

Use what you know. Don't worry about what you don't know.

Michael Shurtleff

Connection is a used but sometimes not much understood term in our industry. People can use it to describe a performance as good or bad. But usually in a lame way to try and make themselves feel like they have seen something nobody else has.

"Wow, they had such a connection."

A bit of a throw-away line if you ask me.

How does the connection work when talking about an actor's method?

Our performances rely on instinct and impulse. To get these impulsive reactions that translate well to the screen, we need to be connected somewhat to our environment and fellow actors.

I said our environment, because when we are in an acting training space, there isn't much about our environment that will serve the truth of our scene so effectively. Instead, we need to transfer and focus our attention on connecting with our fellow actors.

But once we are on a film set, it is uber-simple, easy and natural for our senses to connect with our environment because we will genuinely find ourselves in a believable location that will enhance our performance through belief.

However, our connection with our fellow actors is of prime importance above all.

Why is this method section of the Trinity not in the application section? It is an aspect of your performance whereby you need to psychologically enhance the process, even before you hear 'action' from the director.

This is done in various stages of production.

Firstly, a director may think it suitable for actors that need to have 'symmetry' on screen, so they may invest in some social time for those actors to spend time together in the weeks or months up to the shoot.

Effectively, this gets the actors to feel comfortable around each other, which definitely does translate to the screen. But also, without particularly knowing it, the actors start to recognise quirks, behaviours and actions in each other.

The more time they spend around each other, the more they instinctively see and react to these particular personality traits. This then translates to the screen and we get a feeling that these people completely know each other.

This is also done in reverse, whereby characters that shouldn't know each other at all are kept away from each other. However, it just depends on the director and how much truth they want to get on screen.

Another way to adopt a real deep, more intense connection with your fellow actor(s) is through a technique I devised called 'tunnelling'.

When there isn't much connection between two actors, it is because an actor's range of focus is too wide and they are taking in more stimuli than just the person in front of them. So, I get the actors to face each other, focus and look into each other's eyes.

I then tell them to imagine they are both looking into the end of a tube and I get them to imagine they can only see each other. I ask them to ignore everything else in the environment. Once they are both locked into this 'tunnel', I tell them to start to allow 'moments' to pass between them.

If one feels awkward and starts to laugh, that's fine. But the other person must see it and respond. This is all done without talking. As the focus becomes more intense on each other, the actors can see and respond to each other quicker and more clearly.

These quick reactions and the ability to comfortably focus and be aware of each other are effectively what people refer to as a 'connection' between two actors. But it can easily be formed and manifested, and actors understanding relationships between the characters should manipulate connection accordingly.

Chapter 16
Belief (Method)

For me, our job as artists is to serve the story, serve the director and serve the fellow actors. And if you do that, by osmosis, you're serving yourself because you'll get the best out of yourself.

David Oyelowo

Belief is a massively underrated aspect of acting methodology and yet one that has such a massive impact on the truth of our performance.

To begin with, acting is a strange trade-off on your brain. You are saying to your brain: *Okay, so we are going to pretend that we are in this situation*, and then something doesn't reflect the truth of that situation every time.

Your brain says: *Am I meant to keep going when I am in an acting studio, and you're asking me to pretend we are in a church?* Then in the acting studio, we put our focus on the other person rather than the environment, so your brain says to you: *Okay, I can roll with this*. But then, as soon as something comes up again that is slightly unbelievable to your brain, it comes out of the truth.

That whole paragraph, I hope, demonstrates the battle between the actor, the actors' consciousness, their belief and its effect on the truth of the performance.

How can we psychologically manipulate this so we can genuinely have much more belief in what we are doing and therefore create more truth?

Well, I have already mentioned one of them. Suppose we lose one aspect of our truth. For example, the environment or set may not be as truthful as it could be, so you focus on what is real.

A living, breathing person, delivering (hopefully) a believable performance. That is the one constant in a profession where there can be so many variables.

Another example may be 'green-screen' acting. Such a large percentage of green-screen performances are taking place, and it is a trend that will only climb. Actors have had to develop so many tricks to sustain their belief in what they are doing in an environment that merely contains cameras and green backdrops.

So, what can they focus on in this instance? Again, the living, breathing personality(s) is opposite you. There are the props that will be incredibly believable, costumes and finally, your belief in the events and storyline.

This is the important bit and the real 'method' element of the Trinity that we can adapt and manipulate for our performances.

What we have to do is to be very definitive about the events the writer depicts in his writing. The 'given circumstances'. Then, we must manipulate our brains to believe that this particular event is happening genuinely.

This is a personal thing; however, I choose to block out every other element of my environment, focus on the given circumstances and make myself believe it is happening. Try to see images and get the emotions going that you should be feeling on the back of these circumstances.

Once you feel that you have the maximum belief you can muster in your consciousness, you then connect and work with the truthful elements of the scene to maximise your belief and try to ensure that you ignore the unbelievable aspects of your environment to keep the scene as truthful as possible.

Remember, you will only have truthful, instinctive reactions to what you believe is real.

My biggest annoyance in classes comes from actors opening pretend doors, using their hands as phones, passing over objects with nothing in their hands and pretending to knock on doors where actors stamp and knock on an invisible door! I once had someone put a fist above their head and say 'Nee-Naw', pretending to be a damned ambulance!

How can we maintain belief in this type of behaviour? Whilst learning or in an audition, close the door if there isn't one to use, get your mobile phone out, go outside the room and knock for all I care. Just stop with any element of pretence!

Help your brain maintain belief in the circumstances as this leads to you instinctively create the most truthful responses and therefore, the most truthful scene.

Chapter 17
Aesthetics (Method)

My job is usually to express emotion as freely as possible.

Meryl Streep

This particular subject always makes me think of the conversation I find myself in with actors about Johnny Depp. When we talk about his seemingly diverse range of characters, yet his particular preference to only ever show one aspect of his personality, his 'child'.

So, can he play a huge array of characters or not? I will let the debate rumble on without my input at this stage. However, I want you to notice something that Johnny Depp is incredibly good at. The root of screen acting is not lying to a camera.

So, if you attempt to take on a personality trait you genuinely don't have, you will struggle to appear truthful; however, once rooted in a personality trait, we have a licence to play around with aesthetics.

Aesthetics are the outer layer of an actor that we manufacture to lift the writer's character from the page.

Aesthetics include:

* Accents
* Languages

- * Mannerisms
- * Costume
- * Make-up
- * Movement
- * Voice
- * Skills
- * Combat

As you can imagine, these are all the bits the old-school stage actor gets very excited about. However, under the conditions of camera work, a progressive actor will ensure that every one of these aesthetics will be as real as possible.

Spending time in this method element, doing research and practice and getting these elements fully correct. Or certainly, that should be the aim.

I was lucky enough to have worked with an amazing, Golden Globe-winning actress called Ruth Wilson on the set of the Clio Barnard project, *Dark River*. It was determined that she had to be able to shear sheep, as if she had done this all her life in order to make this look aesthetically correct to the viewing audience.

Ruth spent three months before the shoot working on the aesthetics she would have to add to her performance. This included a very strange dialect to her, which in this instance, was what she was working on with me.

It was a very rare rural form of the Yorkshire dialect, and I have to say, she was amazing. When watching the film, and I urge you to, it takes a little while for you to tune into the dialect and get used to being part of the landscape, but this draws you into their world. This is the effect that Clio Barnard ultimately strives for in her works.

This is the lengths that actors go to in order to get this incredibly important element of their performance correct. It is so important and yet, it is also an incredibly dangerous part for an actor.

Our impulse in going towards our own wants and wishes can come out in this stage, and it is of prime importance that we establish once again that all of these decisions around the aesthetics that you develop over the top of your rooted personality trait/archetype should be based primarily on the writer's intention and the evidence thereof.

We must always defer to the writer. In the example above, I was lucky that Clio Barnard, as well as directing, was also the writer. Therefore, any decision around the dialect in my corner of this production would be deferred directly to her.

You would also find that all other departments dealing with different elements of aesthetics would be doing similar; therefore, keeping to this basic tenet of ensuring the writer's intention is paramount.

So, think of these elements as the outer layer. Work incredibly hard on these elements, particularly focusing on working so hard that they come across as truthfully as possible.

Chapter 18
Behavioural Practice (Method)

An ounce of behaviour is worth a pound of words.

Sanford Meisner

Behaviour is the most important aspect of acting. It's the reason that when we are ill, and we maybe try and drift off to sleep with the TV on mute, we still appear to know exactly what's happening in the TV show.

The actors tell the story through their behaviour. The aspect of our acting is exciting and improvisational and should be our main focus. Why? Because everything follows our behaviour, including the way we say our lines. As well as this, 93% of communication is non-verbal. This is why lines take a back seat.

I have got you to imagine some behavioural choices you would expect yourself to make based on the writer's evidence of the circumstances and events. Again, this is not so you can 'choreograph' these into the scene. This is so that you can have a head full of ideas that your instinct can 'grab' when it chooses.

An effective method for warming up this aspect of making creative, exciting, yet instinctive brave choices goes as follows:

Once you have studied the script and have a good idea of the circumstances and writer's intention, start to neutrally walk around a space. Then, ensure you have your 'head full of ideas' from your 'preparation' element of the Trinity.

Start to believe in the circumstances of the scene, start to think about your character's emotional start-point, objective or whatever particular combination of the Trinity you have prepared, and then as you move around the space, start to engage with these behavioural choices. Let them come out instinctively. Follow every instinct. Never question your instinct; just follow.

Jack Nicolson is amazing at this particular discipline and mixes it with instinct incredibly well. His method is to follow any impulse he gets and go as far as it takes. He talks about how sometimes he looks up and baffles the crew.

To which the director shouts, "Cut! Next Take." However, sometimes he strikes absolute gold, which makes the final cut. He is such a brave, behaviour-led actor.

So, as you move around the space in this particular warm-up exercise, you can warm up these particular behaviours, and if this was on a film set, you should be doing this just before you hear 'action'. This should be your method.

A quick mistake that actors make regularly is they appear to think that the scene begins with the words and ends with the words. It doesn't. I have actors finish the words and then turn to the camera, expecting to hear 'Cut'.

The behaviour and the rolling camera should carry on. The scene is still going and being recorded regardless! Because acting is behaviour, the words just come along for the ride.

Also, at the beginning of a scene, when you hear 'action', actors should start with behaviour and wait for 'instinct' to take them into the words. 'Action' does not mean we say our first line.

'Action' means we start our behaviour around the scene. The editor would want to murder you as there wouldn't be any space between the director shouting action and the first line.

Actors make the mistake of spending all their time focused on the lines and no time on their behaviour. How the lines are articulated will always follow the behaviour, so whatever your behaviour is doing in one moment will affect how the line is said.

So, there is no point standing in front of the mirror deciding how you will say each line. The best thing to do is learn your lines instinctively, then prepare and then practice your behaviours instinctively and allow the lines to come out through the behaviours you are exhibiting. It will always be so much more truthful in the end.

Part 3
Application

Summary

Everything an actor needs to do after they hear 'action' and where they need to put their focus in order to deliver their best scene.

Delivering the performance—focus after 'action'

The **application** stage is where all the work from **preparation** and **method** comes to life. This is the moment when the cameras roll and the actor steps fully into the scene. Now, it's time to trust the work you've done and focus on delivering a truthful, engaging performance.

In this phase, your goal is to be fully present, responding naturally to the moment whilst staying true to the **writer's intention.**

The **application** phase is about **focus**—knowing where to direct your attention during the scene to ensure that your performance remains grounded, authentic and impactful.

This is not the time to second-guess your preparation; instead, it's about immersing yourself in the scene, allowing everything you've worked on to flow through you.

Chapter 19
Listening (Application)

Listening is not merely hearing. Listening is reacting. Listening is being affected by what you hear. Listening is active.

Michael Shurtleff

The application section of the Trinity is what we do after we hear 'action'. The things we need to do during the performance. The mind-set or 'state' we need to adopt to maximise our performance.

If it was up to the late Alan Rickman, this would be the only chapter of any book on acting. He famously said he considered acting as 'being paid for people to watch him listen'. He also said, "All I want to see from an actor is the intensity and accuracy of their listening."

I fully endorse the importance of listening in acting as being incredibly important. We are not 'actors'; we are 're-actors'. What are we constantly reacting to? Stimuli. The main stimuli are our fellow actors.

Our hearing is the sense we constantly have in operation, bringing us the most information. If you have your focus on reacting to what you hear, you have no choice but to be in a reactive state.

In order to 'exist' within a scene and be as truthful as possible, we need to rely on our instincts. Which, in essence, is our subconscious brain. Our subconscious brain reacts instinctively to what we hear.

In classes, I constantly watch an actor that is, in their conscious brain, not listening at all. They are waiting to deliver their line. They have practised their line and decided how they think it sounds best.

When it comes out, it is so far removed from the line their fellow actor has just delivered that it sounds like it has been plucked from nowhere. The scene then feels contrived. It feels like the two actors may as well be in two different rooms.

So, as soon as we hear action, we need to adopt a position in our subconscious brain. We must set our ears into listening mode rather than forcing instinctive responses. We need to trust that they are happening. The more detail you listen to, the more response your subconscious creates.

To get my actors to understand the importance of listening, I use this particular sentence:

'I never said they stole my money.'

This is an incredibly interesting sentence because highlighting one word in this sentence creates a different meaning every time. You have to listen incredibly intently to hear which word the actor highlights and create meaning thereafter.

However, even though this is merely an exercise, this happens in most sentences that are spoken. We all choose to use our tone and pace to highlight certain words in sentences to create meaning.

We pick up on this in everyday life and respond appropriately. For some reason, when acting, we need to work a bit harder on this and ensure that we put ourselves in this mind-set.

This is where we get a truthful performance from and get the impression that the actors in the scene are in the same 'moment' together. Also, the audience is potentially listening just as intently as the actor.

They can tell if you have missed the meaning of the line you have just heard. This is one of the main reasons that an audience fails to believe your performance, as they expect you to react to the same meaning they have heard, and if you don't react to the same information, it ends up with your performance being somewhat removed from the scene.

So, listening is a mind-set, a place for your conscious mind to focus that is not your lines and the way you have rehearsed and decided you want to say them. If you find yourself doing this, learn your lines instinctively and put your focus on reaching out with your senses. One of the most important of which is listening.

Chapter 20
Seeing (Application)

I'm curious about other people. That's the essence of my acting. I'm interested in what it would be like to be you.

Meryl Streep

However, the obvious next step to listening needs to be dealt with slightly differently. Please keep in mind the mind-set element and the idea that it is of prime importance that you focus your conscious brain away from your lines and onto your senses that you require your subconscious brain to be instinctive to react to.

Another main sense is your vision and what you see.

I do an experiment with actors in workshops, whereby I get one person to watch another person as they watch me speak. They notice that actually when I'm talking to them, they never actually take their eyes off me as I'm talking to them. Then, when I mention it, the actor being watched suddenly feels awkward and starts looking away.

So, generally speaking, we focus on each other when talking around 95% of the time. This is something that doesn't always feel 100% natural, but to engage in a truthful scene, it is something that we need to ensure we do.

I once had to turn around the fortunes of an actor on set quickly. I had a couple of minutes literally with them, as the director felt their performance wasn't where it needed to be. I could see that the actor was very much in their conscious brain, trying to think of the lines, detached from the scene at hand and putting themselves under awful pressure.

In the two minutes I had, I decided to say the following:

"Over-look, over-listen and just let the lines drop out of your mouth."

All of a sudden, the actor delivered an incredible turnaround. They were subtle, real and had an incredible demeanour as their personality came across. The director turned to me with a look of 'How did you manage that!'

How did this work?

As I mentioned, the actor in question was stuck in their conscious brain and not existing in the circumstances. Getting them to 'over-look' and 'over-listen' gave the actor something for their conscious brain to do, leaving their instinct free to deal with reacting to the stimuli that came from what he could hear and see.

Allowing the words to 'drop out of his mouth' gave him an idea that he just needed to trust that the lines would just happen as a by-product of instinct, without him over-performing them.

This made him deliver an instinctive personality and instinct/impulse is personality, which was very much missing from his original performance. So, 'looking' and 'seeing' are incredibly important in the same way as 'listening' is.

What level of detail should you see?

I say to my actors they should see every blink! Your subconscious is a machine that needs feeding. The more you feed it, the more instinct comes through in your performance. The more instinct, the more truthful your performance is.

I will end this section by giving a piece of advice I give to anyone who will listen.

In order to be the best at anything you want, you only have to do two things:

1) You have to see more detail than anyone else.
2) You have to respond to that detail better.

Acting is no different. Point 1 is listening and seeing, and point 2 is your instincts.

Chapter 21
Bravery (Application)

I'm a skilled professional actor. Whether or not I've any talent is beside the point.

Michael Caine

Actors need to be incredibly brave, but what is bravery? Bravery is being scared, fearful and uncomfortable, but not letting it stop you from doing what you must. The biggest misconception in our industry is that actors are a special breed that don't feel these emotions, and because they don't appear to feel scared, fearful or uncomfortable, they must be brave. In fact, it's the biggest act of all!

They feel all of these things but utilise these emotions to appear vulnerable on camera, enhance their performance, and give them the focus and energy to do a particularly good job.

I constantly say to my actors that when we act, we go into our fear responses. Freeze, flight and fight. These particular fear responses manifest slightly differently in actors if you learn what to look for.

FREEZE—Actors can literally freeze and not do anything. Freeze on set, freeze on stage. This also manifests itself in procrastinating, being laboured in your efforts and being absent from everyone.

FLIGHT—This manifests itself in actors in some very strange ways. Have you ever seen an actor that 'over-giggles' on set? They are running away from what they know they have to do. They would rather giggle about it than confront it.

Also, when the actor is running away, they ask lots of questions. "Do you mean—? Do you want me to—?" They have heard you for the first time. However, the more they ask questions about your instruction or what they inevitably have to do, the more they get to delay it.

This is a pure flight reaction. I have also literally just seen people run away! Physically! They feel so uncomfortable that they want to escape the situation quickly.

FIGHT—This is the bravery we require. This is what actors need to be able to train themselves to do for their careers. Learn to feel every single one of the aforementioned emotions, but fight to pursue your task despite these emotions. This is what bravery is.

I am asking you to utilise your subconscious and follow your instincts and impulses. This can feel wild and out of control at times, and it takes real bravery to follow an impulse to the end without hesitation.

However, as we see from some of the best film moments in cinema history, our commitment to this practice creates some amazing, truthful, real and exciting moments. It takes huge bravery on behalf of the actors, and that's why I always feel that the best actors are the bravest.

Strangely, when you see interviews with some of the absolute best actors on the planet, they appear shy. Daniel Day-Lewis and Johnny Depp are my two examples. However, they produce amazing performances on screen.

The reason that shy, apparently awkward people can create such magic is bravery. Feeling the fear and discomfort, but not letting it stop you from doing what you need to do and using these emotions to add something to your performance rather than inhibit it.

My final point on this subject is this:

Actors need to train themselves to be comfortable with being uncomfortable.

Chapter 22
Behaviour (Application)

I think your self emerges more clearly over time.

Meryl Streep

So, in the first part of the Trinity, we looked at getting as many behavioural options as possible prepared and ready. In the second part of the Trinity, we even practised some of these behaviours and effectively warmed them up.

Once you have heard 'action', the worst situation you want to be in is that you are focused on the lines and how you say them, and you are in a place in your head whereby you are searching for the lines.

You need to learn the lines incredibly well and in a way that they become instinctive, so that you don't need to search for the lines in your head. They roll off the tongue.

So, where does your focus need to be?

Your focus needs to be on creating the focus needed on your circumstances, the other person, and how you feel and from this, you will feel the need to respond.

Here is where you respond with a behaviour.

You have programmed your mind with plenty of ideas. You have warmed up and already played out some of these behaviours in the method element of the Trinity. This will help you be able to access these actions and behaviours quickly when you feel the need to react to a behaviour or an action. This physically manifested response will direct how your lines come out and fuse to sound and look incredibly truthful.

Just remember, you have 'green-lit' all of the behaviours you have prepared. You have told yourself that if the moment arises and you feel an impulse, you can do any one of the behaviours that you have prepared. This will result in an exciting and dynamic performance of the scene that audiences won't be able to take their eyes off.

The main thing to really understand in the application section of the Trinity around behaviour is that your behaviour takes precedence over your lines, and you must allow your lines and the way you say your lines to follow your behaviour in every moment of the scene.

Another thing worth noting is that actors, when focused on the lines, seem to think that the scene begins when the lines begin and end when the lines end.

The scene can begin anytime, even before you hear 'action' because you can start your behaviour anytime. Actors that are considered 'method' in the convoluted sense do this and can confuse people on set who don't understand their process.

Actors also sometimes make the mistake of turning to the camera or finishing before 'cut' just because they've finished their lines and this is a huge mistake.

Also, remember that if you are focused on the behaviour, you won't be frightened of pauses. Actors that seem to rush scripts are scared of pauses as they feel like nothing is happening.

This is why actors focused on behaviour effortlessly move through scenes, committing to pauses and creating some amazing moments in their behaviour when there is no dialogue. These are the moments where you see an actor performing and focusing correctly.

Chapter 23
Tasks Delivery (Application)

Acting is all about honesty.
If you can fake that, you've got it made.

George Burns

Now and again in a scene, you will notice that your character is carrying out a physical or mental task within the scene. If this is the case, ensure that you fully commit to the task. When you hear 'action', you ensure that your focus is on this task.

Once you have identified a task that your character is pursuing, deal with it similarly to your prepared behaviours. Make sure you put your mental focus here and allow your lines to follow the task.

If your task is to build a wall, the movement and toil of this task will affect how you say your lines. If you are running, it will certainly affect how you will deliver your lines.

If it is a mental task, like you are trying to work out a complex maths problem, the focus on the problem will affect how you will interact with anyone speaking to you.

I see that the biggest mistake in this area is that actors stop the task to deliver their line and then do a bit more of it afterwards. This is a curse of an actor who is purely focused on lines.

Another thing that I constantly see with tasks is just how committed an actor can be to the said task. I see many people use a mobile phone in scenes. However, I don't see them 'Face unlock' their phone, look through their contacts and finally press call on the person they wish to call.

This highlights the extent of commitment to the tasks required. In a close-up, on screen, these things get noticed. You need to commit to any task fully, as this then affects how you say your lines and the belief in your performance for you and the viewing audience.

Chapter 24
Beats and Tactics (Application)

Find in yourself those human things which are universal.

Sanford Meisner

This is a very advanced technique, so I've included it last. It takes a little while to train yourself to follow this particular performance pattern, but actors that work at it and train themselves to do it create awe-inducing performances.

So, we work out our objective for the scene and then gather some verbs that represent the tactics we are to employ within the scene to achieve the said objective. However, the question is 'when' to change tactics?

The answer is quite simple, whenever our character, you have a new thought.

So, the first step in this technique is to ensure that we split our script into every new thought. Denoted with a '/' representing a beat or a period of thought.

(I committed this little section on splitting up your script with beats, as I wanted to deal with this subject all at once because it takes much understanding. However, you could do this part during the preparation stage of the Trinity.)

Once you have added this to your whole script, realise that every time your character has a new thought, you also need to have a new thought. In these moments, you change tactics. Suppose you genuinely attempt a new tactic on every one of your characters' new thoughts. In that case, the effect will give you an incredibly varied, interesting, exciting and surprisingly truthful version of the script.

I get my actors to close their eyes and listen to me teach them. My objective is for them to learn. I have various different tactics with my communication and behaviour to achieve this.

When they listen carefully, they can hear that I pause on a new thought and then change direction to a new tactic. They can hear the new pace of speech and the change in tone. The difference in expression, attitude and demeanour.

But what makes you decide on which tactic to change to on every thought?

The other person, the circumstances, your thoughts and your emotion.

If you make yourself fully aware of everything you see, hear, think and feel, your instincts and impulses will work overtime, and you will very quickly decide on which direction to go.

Game of Thrones is an amazing example of this technique. On paper, *Game of Thrones* should not work; it is effectively an old-fashioned chamber play put on screen. Characters are having 6-minute conversations in a throne room. Due to the strength of its acting, it has since become the most popular TV show in the world. Why?

Because of this technique.

A scene between Varys (Conleth Hill) and Littlefinger (Aiden Gillen) that I am particularly drawn to is an epic scene in front of the iron throne (*The Climb*-Season 3, Episode 6).

They hardly move, but it is one of the most fixating and amazing scenes I have ever witnessed.

It is like a game of tennis. They both have an objective. They both are living that objective. One actor throws a tactic at the other actor, and the other actor reads that tactic, makes an instant impulsive decision, and decides which tactic to send in response.

Even if the actors changed tactics mid-sentence, it is based upon the expression or demeanour of the other actor. This is what amazing actors can do. This is how best to employ this technique.

It doesn't matter what scene you are involved in; this technique will elevate it. However, this takes practice. Start slowly in a rehearsal phase, maybe just exploring from beat to beat, then speed it up until it becomes instinctive.

Try and change gear with every thought, and the results will astound you. Not only will it keep the other actor on their toes, it will keep you truthful and focused in all the right areas.

Epilogue—Your Trinity

Anyone can be an actor. You have to get rid of your limiting beliefs and have a genuine desire to take so much action on your career that success becomes inevitable.

Matt Zina

So, there you have it. I have poured my heart and soul into this book of my work and technique development over the last 20+ years of coaching emerging and professional actors.

But even though you now know the Trinity Acting Method and all the individual methods contained within, how do you implement it to improve your acting?

You need to use as many of these micro-methods as possible to create an amazing scene; however, you can't use all of them.

So, how do you assess which techniques you use and which you leave out and now that you understand the three parts of the Trinity, how do you actually use it in practice?

Here is a step-by-step breakdown of how to apply the method to improve your acting:

1. Review the Script:

Begin by diving deep into the script using the preparation techniques outlined in chapter 4. Look for clues about the

scene type, the writer's intentions and the overall context of the story. Consider the **director, writer** and **production house** style. Ask yourself, *what will this scene look like?* What is the scene's focus? How does it contribute to the story? This step is about understanding the **output** needed from the scene.

2. Select Your Techniques:

Once you've understood the scene, assess which **preparation, method** and **application** techniques will help you achieve the desired result. Not every technique will be relevant for every scene. Focus on the ones that will bring out the best version of the story.

3. Commit Fully:

After selecting your version of the **Trinity,** commit fully to the process. Use the selected techniques to serve the **writer's intention** and execute the scene with absolute truth. Trust your preparation and method work, and bring it all to life in the application phase.

I hope this book and this acting method help you achieve everything you dream of in this industry. It will continue to be one of the most amazing industries.

With the correct mind-set, business strategy and business knowledge, plus a good knowledge and application of the Trinity Acting Method, you now have every tool available to succeed.

Ready?

Acting Practitioners

My thought process has always been, I'm excited to show you what my version of this story would look like. You're going to be able to get a little condensed show. That took the pressure off getting the job.

Tituss Burgess

Below, you'll find a list of some of the most well-known acting practitioners who have left their mark on the world of acting. Some of them I've referenced in this book, and some I haven't, but I genuinely believe every actor should take the time to read and explore different acting techniques throughout their career.

And, if I may add a personal touch, seeing my name alongside these incredible practitioners honestly gives me shivers down my spine. It's been my mission to rub shoulders with the greats, and I hope that one day, this book and my work with actors will truly place me among them.

1. **Konstantin Stanislavsky (1863-1938)**
    - **Famous for:** The **Stanislavsky System,** often called 'Method Acting'.
    - **Key Contributions:** Stanislavsky emphasised naturalistic performance, emotional truth and the

importance of the actor's inner experience. He developed techniques like **emotional memory, objective-based acting** and the use of **given circumstances** to create believable characters.
- **Key Works:** *An Actor Prepares, Building a Character, Creating a Role.*
- **Further Reading:** *Stanislavski in Rehearsal* by Vasili Toporkov.

2. **Sanford Meisner (1905-1997)**
   - **Famous for:** The **Meisner Technique.**
   - **Key Contributions:** Meisner focused on **living truthfully under imaginary circumstances.** His technique emphasised **repetition exercises** to help actors respond instinctively and emotionally in the moment, enhancing spontaneity and genuine reactions in performance.
   - **Key Works:** *Sanford Meisner on Acting.*
   - **Further Reading:** *The Actor's Art and Craft* by William Esper and Damon D'Marco.

3. **Stella Adler (1901-1992)**
   - **Famous for:** The **Adler Technique,** an offshoot of Stanislavsky's method.
   - **Key Contributions:** Adler believed in using **imagination** and the **power of circumstance** rather than personal emotional memory. She emphasised **script analysis,** expanding the actor's knowledge of history and literature, and creating a character from external circumstances.

- **Key Works:** *The Art of Acting.*
- **Further Reading:** *Stella Adler on America's Master Play-wrights.*

4. **Lee Strasberg (1901-1982)**
   - **Famous for:** The **Strasberg Method** or **Method Acting.**
   - **Key Contributions:** Building on Stanislavsky's work, Strasberg focused on **emotional memory** and the actor's ability to use personal experiences to inform their character's emotional life. His technique is often associated with deep, immersive character work.
   - **Key Works:** *A Dream of Passion: The Development of the Method.*
   - **Further Reading:** *The Lee Strasberg Notes* edited by Lola Cohen.

5. **Uta Hagen (1919-2004)**
   - **Famous for:** The **Hagen Technique.**
   - **Key Contributions:** Hagen's approach was rooted in **realism** and the actor's **emotional connection** to the character. She emphasised working with **objectives, inner thoughts** and personal connections to the character's circumstances to create a truthful performance.
   - **Key Works:** *Respect for Acting, a Challenge for the Actor.*
   - **Further Reading:** *Uta Hagen's Acting Class: The DVDs* by Uta Hagen.

6. **Michael Chekhov (1891-1955)**
   - **Famous for:** The **Chekhov Technique.**
   - **Key Contributions:** Chekhov focused on using the **psychological gesture** to unlock a character's inner life and physical expression. His approach emphasised **imagination** and **physicality** as tools for emotional expression, often working from the outside in.
   - **Key Works:** *To the Actor: On the Technique of Acting.*
   - **Further Reading:** *On the Technique of Acting* by Michael Chekhov, edited by Mel Gordon.

7. **Jerzy Grotowski (1933-1999)**
   - **Famous for: Physical theatre** and the **Poor Theatre** movement.
   - **Key Contributions:** Grotowski stripped away traditional theatrical elements—such as elaborate sets and costumes—focusing instead on the actor's **physicality** and their relationship with the audience. His work pushed the boundaries of how an actor can express emotion through movement.
   - **Key Works:** *Towards a Poor Theatre.*
   - **Further Reading:** *Grotowski's Empty Room* by Lisa Wolford and Richard Schechner.

8. **Antonin Artaud (1896-1948)**
   - **Famous for: Theatre of Cruelty.**
   - **Key Contributions:** Artaud's theories were avant-garde, emphasising the need to **shock the**

audience and disrupt conventional theatre. He focused on **extreme physicality** and the use of **visual and sensory elements** to communicate deeper human emotions and experiences.
- **Key Works:** *The Theatre and Its Double.*
- **Further Reading:** *Artaud Anthology* edited by Jack Hirschman.

9. **Bertolt Brecht (1898-1956)**
   - **Famous for: Epic Theatre.**
   - **Key Contributions:** Brecht believed theatre should inspire **critical thinking** rather than emotional manipulation. His techniques, like **alienation** (Verfremdungseffekt), encouraged actors to make the audience aware they are watching a play, often breaking the fourth wall to promote social and political reflection.
   - **Key Works:** *Brecht on Theatre.*
   - **Further Reading:** *Brecht in Practice: Theatre, Theory and Performance* by David Barnett.

10. **Viola Spolin (1906-1994)**
    - **Famous for:** The **mother of improvisation.**
    - **Key Contributions:** Spolin developed techniques to **free the actor's spontaneity** through improvisational games. Her work had a huge influence on American theatre and comedy, especially in the development of improv.
    - **Key Works:** *Improvisation for the Theatre.*

- **Further Reading:** *Theatre Games for the Lone Actor* by Viola Spolin.

11. **Anne Bogart (1951-present)**
    - **Famous for:** The **Viewpoints Technique.**
    - **Key Contributions:** Bogart's **Viewpoints** is a method for training performers and creating movement through an actor's awareness of **time, space and movement.** It helps actors respond physically to the moment and build ensemble work.
    - **Key Works:** *The Viewpoints Book.*
    - **Further Reading:** A *Director Prepares: Seven Essays on Art and Theatre* by Anne Bogart.

12. **Augusto Boal (1931-2009)**
    - **Famous for: Theatre of the Oppressed.**
    - **Key Contributions:** Boal developed theatre as a means of promoting **social and political change,** encouraging interaction between performers and the audience. His techniques include **Forum Theatre** and **Image Theatre,** where the audience actively participates in shaping the performance.
    - **Key Works:** *Theatre of the Oppressed.*
    - **Further Reading:** *Games for Actors and Non-Actors* by Augusto Boal.

13. **Matt Zina (1983-Present)**
    - **Famous for:** The **Trinity Acting Method.**

- **Key Contributions:** Matt Zina developed the **Trinity Acting Method,** which emphasises the **writer's intention** as the foundation for a truthful performance. His method is divided into three parts: **Preparation, method** and **application,** focusing on analysing the script, preparing emotionally and physically, and delivering the performance with full commitment. Zina's approach is particularly effective in **screen acting** where subtlety and truth are essential.
- **Key Works:** *The Trinity Acting Method.*
- **Further Reading:** Explore more at mzacting.com.

Glossary

1) **Human Emotions.**
   - Admiration
   - Adoration
   - Aesthetic Appreciation
   - Amusement
   - Anxiety
   - Awe
   - Awkwardness
   - Boredom
   - Calmness
   - Confusion
   - Craving
   - Disgust
   - Empathetic pain
   - Entrancement
   - Envy
   - Excitement
   - Fear
   - Horror
   - Interest
   - Joy

- Nostalgia
- Romance
- Sadness
- Satisfaction
- Sexual desire
- Sympathy
- Triumph

2) Common Objectives.

To Help Me
To Save Me
To Go Away
To Understand
To Play
To Bite
To Get on Side
To Get on Board
To Crack
To Break
To Crumble
To Surrender
To Laugh
To Smile
To Battle
To Be Reassured
To Snap
To Be Wound up
To Man Up
To Submit
To Melt
To Back Down

To Squirm
To Blush
To Get a Grip
To Like Me
To Love Me

3) **Human Characteristics**
1. Sincere
2. Honest
3. Understanding
4. Loyal
5. Truthful
6. Trustworthy
7. Intelligent
8. Dependable
9. Open-Minded
10. Thoughtful
11. Wise
12. Considerate
13. Good-Natured
14. Reliable
15. Mature
16. Warm
17. Earnest
18. Kind
19. Friendly
20. Kind-hearted
21. Happy
22. Clean
23. Interesting
24. Unselfish

25. Good-humoured
26. Honourable
27. Humorous
28. Responsible
29. Cheerful
30. Trustful
31. Warm-hearted
32. Broad-minded
33. Gentle
34. Well-spoken
35. Educated
36. Reasonable
37. Companionable
38. Likeable
39. Trusting
40. Clever
41. Pleasant
42. Courteous
43. Quick-witted
44. Tactful
45. Helpful
46. Appreciative
47. Imaginative
48. Outstanding
49. Self-disciplined
50. Brilliant
51. Enthusiastic
52. Level-headed
53. Polite
54. Original
55. Smart

56. Forgiving
57. Sharp-witted
58. Well-Read
59. Ambitious
60. Bright
61. Respectful
62. Efficient
63. Good-tempered
64. Grateful
65. Conscientious
66. Resourceful
67. Alert
68. Good
69. Witty
70. Clear-headed
71. Kindly
72. Admirable
73. Patient
74. Talented
75. Perceptive
76. Spirited
77. Sportsmanlike
78. Well-mannered
79. Cooperative
80. Ethical
81. Intellectual
82. Versatile
83. Capable
84. Courageous
85. Constructive
86. Productive

87. Progressive
88. Individualistic
89. Observant
90. Ingenious
91. Lively
92. Neat
93. Punctual
94. Logical
95. Prompt
96. Accurate
97. Sensible
98. Creative
99. Self-reliant
100. Tolerant
101. Amusing
102. Clean-cut
103. Generous
104. Sympathetic
105. Energetic
106. High-spirited
107. Self-controlled
108. Tender
109. Active
110. Independent
111. Respectable
112. Inventive
113. Wholesome
114. Congenial
115. Cordial
116. Experienced
117. Attentive

118. Cultured
119. Frank
120. Purposeful
121. Decent
122. Diligent
123. Realist
124. Eager
125. Poised
126. Competent
127. Realistic
128. Amiable
129. Optimistic
130. Vigorous
131. Entertaining
132. Adventurous
133. Vivacious
134. Composed
135. Relaxed
136. Romantic
137. Proficient
138. Rational
139. Skilful
140. Enterprising
141. Gracious
142. Able
143. Nice
144. Agreeable
145. Skilled
146. Curious
147. Modern
148. Charming

149. Sociable
150. Modest
151. Decisive
152. Humble
153. Tidy
154. Popular
155. Upright
156. Literary
157. Practical
158. Light-hearted
159. Well-bred
160. Refined
161. Self-confident
162. Cool-headed
163. Studious
164. Adventuresome
165. Discreet
166. Informal
167. Thorough
168. Exuberant
169. Inquisitive
170. Easy-going
171. Outgoing
172. Self-sufficient
173. Casual
174. Consistent
175. Moral
176. Self-assured
177. Untiring
178. Hopeful
179. Calm

180. Strong-minded
181. Positive
182. Confident
183. Artistic
184. Precise
185. Scientific
186. Orderly
187. Social
188. Direct
189. Careful
190. Candid
191. Comical
192. Obliging
193. Self-critical
194. Fashionable
195. Religious
196. Soft-hearted
197. Dignified
198. Philosophical
199. Idealistic
200. Soft-spoken
201. Disciplined
202. Serious
203. Definite
204. Convincing
205. Persuasive
206. Obedient
207. Quick
208. Sophisticated
209. Thrifty
210. Sentimental

211. Objective
212. Nonconforming
213. Righteous
214. Mathematical
215. Meditative
216. Fearless
217. Systematic
218. Subtle
219. Normal
220. Daring
221. Middle-class
222. Lucky
223. Proud
224. Sensitive
225. Moralistic
226. Talkative
227. Excited
228. Moderate
229. Satirical
230. Prudent
231. Reserved
232. Persistent
233. Meticulous
234. Unconventional
235. Deliberate
236. Painstaking
237. Bold
238. Suave
239. Cautious
240. Innocent
241. Inoffensive

242. Shrewd
243. Methodical
244. Nonchalant
245. Self-contented
246. Perfectionist
247. Forward
248. Excitable
249. Outspoken
250. Prideful
251. Quiet
252. Impulsive
253. Aggressive
254. Changeable
255. Conservative
256. Shy
257. Hesitant
258. Unpredictable
259. Solemn
260. Blunt
261. Self-righteous
262. Average
263. Discriminating
264. Emotional
265. Unlucky
266. Bashful
267. Self-concerned
268. Authoritative
269. Lonesome
270. Restless
271. Choosy
272. Self-possessed

273. Naive
274. Opportunist
275. Theatrical
276. Unsophisticated
277. Impressionable
278. Ordinary
279. Strict
280. Sceptical
281. Extravagant
282. Forceful
283. Cunning
284. Inexperienced
285. Unmethodical
286. Daredevil
287. Wordy
288. Daydreamer
289. Conventional
290. Materialistic
291. Self-satisfied
292. Rebellious
293. Eccentric
294. Opinionated
295. Stern
296. Lonely
297. Dependent
298. Unsystematic
299. Self-conscious
300. Undecided
301. Resigned
302. Clownish
303. Anxious

304. Conforming
305. Critical
306. Conformist
307. Radical
308. Dissatisfied
309. Old-fashioned
310. Meek
311. Frivolous
312. Discontented
313. Troubled
314. Irreligious
315. Overcautious
316. Silent
317. Tough
318. Ungraceful
319. Argumentative
320. Withdrawing
321. Uninquisitive
322. Forgetful
323. Inhibited
324. Unskilled
325. Crafty
326. Passive
327. Immodest
328. Unpopular
329. Timid
330. Spendthrift
331. Temperamental
332. Gullible
333. Indecisive
334. Silly

335. Submissive
336. Studious
337. Preoccupied
338. Tense
339. Fearful
340. Unromantic
341. Absent-minded
342. Impractical
343. Withdrawn
344. Unadventurous
345. Sarcastic
346. Sad
347. Unemotional
348. Worrying
349. High-strung
350. Unoriginal
351. Unpoised
352. Compulsive
353. Worrier
354. Demanding
355. Unhappy
356. Indifferent
357. Uncultured
358. Clumsy
359. Insecure
360. Unentertaining
361. Imitative
362. Melancholy
363. Mediocre
364. Obstinate
365. Unhealthy

366. Headstrong
367. Nervous
368. Non-confident
369. Stubborn
370. Unimaginative
371. Downhearted
372. Unobservant
373. Inconsistent
374. Unpunctual
375. Unindustrious
376. Disturbed
377. Superstitious
378. Frustrated
379. Illogical
380. Rash
381. Unenthusiastic
382. Inaccurate
383. Non-inquisitive
384. Unarguable
385. Jumpy
386. Possessive
387. Purposeless
388. Moody
389. Unenterprising
390. Unintellectual
391. Unwise
392. Oversensitive
393. Inefficient
394. Reckless
395. Pompous
396. Uncongenial

397. Untidy
398. Unaccommodating
399. Noisy
400. Squeamish
401. Cynical
402. Angry
403. Listless
404. Uninspiring
405. Unintelligent
406. Domineering
407. Scolding
408. Depressed
409. Unboiling
410. Pessimistic
411. Inattentive
412. Boisterous
413. Suspicious
414. Inattentive
415. Overconfident
416. Smug
417. Unsociable
418. Unproductive
419. Wasteful
420. Fickle
421. Neglectful
422. Short-tempered
423. Hot-headed
424. Unsocial
425. Envious
426. Overcritical
427. Scheming

428. Sly
429. Weak
430. Foolhardy
431. Immature
432. Dominating
433. Showy
434. Sloppy
435. Unsympathetic
436. Uncompromising
437. Hot-tempered
438. Neurotic
439. Unsporting
440. Finicky
441. Resentful
442. Unruly
443. Fault-finding
444. Messy
445. Misfit
446. Uninteresting
447. Scornful
448. Antisocial
449. Irritable
450. Stingy
451. Tactless
452. Careless
453. Foolish
454. Troublesome
455. Ungracious
456. Negligent
457. Wishy-washy
458. Profane

459. Gloomy
460. Helpless
461. Disagreeable
462. Touchy
463. Irrational
464. Tiresome
465. Disobedient
466. Complaining
467. Lifeless
468. Vain
469. Lazy
470. Unappreciative
471. Maladjusted
472. Aimless
473. Boastful
474. Dull
475. Gossipy
476. Unappealing
477. Hypochondriac
478. Irritating
479. Petty
480. Shallow
481. Deceptive
482. Grouchy
483. Egotistical
484. Meddlesome
485. Uncivil
486. Cold
487. Unsportsmanlike
488. Bossy
489. Unpleasing

490. Cowardly
491. Discourteous
492. Incompetent
493. Childish
494. Superficial
495. Ungrateful
496. Self-conceited
497. Hard-hearted
498. Unfair
499. Irresponsible
500. Prejudiced
501. Bragging
502. Jealous
503. Unpleasant
504. Unreliable
505. Impolite
506. Crude
507. Nosey
508. Humourless
509. Quarrelsome
510. Abusive
511. Distrustful
512. Intolerant
513. Unforgiving
514. Boring
515. Unethical
516. Unreasonable
517. Self-centred
518. Snobbish
519. Unkindly
520. Ill-mannered

521. Ill-tempered
522. Unfriendly
523. Hostile
524. Dislikeable
525. Ultra-critical
526. Offensive
527. Belligerent
528. Underhanded
529. Annoying
530. Disrespectful
531. Loud-mouthed
532. Selfish
533. Narrow-minded
534. Vulgar
535. Heartless
536. Insolent
537. Thoughtless
538. Rude
539. Conceited
540. Greedy
541. Spiteful
542. Insulting
543. Insincere
544. Unkind
545. Untrustworthy
546. Deceitful
547. Dishonourable
548. Malicious
549. Obnoxious
550. Untruthful
551. Dishonest

552. Cruel
553. Mean
554. Phony
555. Liar

4) Archetypes
Actor
Anarchist
Bureaucrat
Caregiver
Companion
Crone
Detective
Diplomat
Dreamer
Fool
God
Healer
Historian
Knight
Magician
Matriarch
Muse
Networker
Patriarch
Poet
Priest
Prophet
Puck
Rebel
Revolutionary

Sadist
Scholar
Seductress
Servant
Side-kick
Storyteller
Thief
Tyrant
Visionary
Wizard
Addict
Artist
Beggar
Child
Coward
Crook
Dictator
Disciple
Eternal
Gala
Goddess
Herald
Innovator
Liberator
Martyr
Midas
Mystic
Nun
Pilgrim
Politician
Prince

- Puppet
- Redeemer
- Robot
- Sage
- Scout
- Seeker
- Settler
- Slave
- Student
- Tramp
- Vampire
- Warrior
- Zombie
- Alchemist
- Avenger
- Bully
- Clown
- Craftsperson
- Damsel
- Dilettante
- Diva
- Evangelist
- Gambler
- Gossip
- Hermit
- Judge
- Lover
- Masochist
- Monk
- Nature Boy/Girl
- Olympian

Pioneer
Predator
Princess
Provocateur
Puritan
Rescuer
Saboteur
Samaritan
Scribe
Seer
Shaman
Spoiler
Teacher
Trickster
Victim
Witch

5) Examples of Modern Archetypes

Bitch
Chav
Influencer
Gay Best Friend
Hipster
Road-man
Non-binary